We Love to Sew

28 Pretty Things to Make:
Jewelry • Headbands • Softies • T-shirts
Pillows • Bags & More

Annabel Wrigley

FunStitch
STUDIO
stitch your art out.

Text copyright © 2013 by Annabel Wrigley

Photography and Artwork copyright © 2013 by C&T Publishing, Inc.

Publisher: Amy Marson

Creative Director: Gailen Runge

Art Director/Book Designer: Kristy Zacharias

Editor: Cynthia Bix

Technical Editors: Carolyn Aune and Amanda Siegfried

Production Coordinator: Zinnia Heinzmann

Production Editor: Alice Mace Nakanishi

Illustrators: Drawings by Peter Dahlquist; Pattern Illustrations by Tim Manibusan

Photography by Kristen Gardner, unless otherwise noted

Published by FunStitch Studio, an imprint of C&T Publishing, Inc., P.O. Box 1456, Lafayette, CA 94549

Library of Congress Cataloging-in-Publication Data

Wrigley, Annabel, 1972-

 We love to sew : 28 pretty things to make: jewelry, headbands, softies, t-shirts, pillows, bags & more / Annabel Wrigley.

    pages cm

  ISBN 978-1-60705-632-4 (soft cover)

1. Sewing--Juvenile literature. 2. Textile crafts--Juvenile literature. 3. Handicraft for girls--Juvenile literature. I. Title.

  TT712.W75 2013

  646'.1--dc23

              2012035169

Printed in China

10 9 8 7 6 5 4

Dedication
For Darren, Ollie, and Ruby

ACKNOWLEDGMENTS

To my amazing husband, Darren, whose infinite encouragement and support has made this entire process a little less terrifying. Your unspoken dedication to making everything easier for me never went unnoticed and will be forever appreciated.

To my creative daughter, Ruby, who has served as constant inspiration to me and has shown me that children are capable of so much more than we give them credit for!

To my extraordinary son, Oliver, who made it his priority every day to ask me how my day was going as I sat in pajamas in front of the computer with bed hair at 3 P.M.

To my amazing and supportive group of friends, old and new, near and far, who have served as sounding boards, therapists, cheer squad, and pit crew. You know who you are, and I love every last one of you.

To Gresh, whose constant love, support, daily messages, and genuine excitement for this project have lifted me up and kept me motivated to keep going even when piles of homework and dirty dishes threatened to take me off track.

To my wonderful family members back home, who have been through this process with me all the way and whom I miss daily.

So many thanks to my agent, Kate McKean, who handled my freak-out emails with patience and understanding, and whose guidance has been invaluable.

Thanks to everyone at C&T for helping me and guiding me in the process of making a beautiful book. To Cynthia Bix, my amazing and calm editor who has never once doubted I could do this even though at times I was not sure. To Diane, Kristy, and Zinnia for understanding my creative vision and letting me run with it. To Carolyn, for helping me make this book easy to use for all the crafty kids out there. And, of course, to acquisitions editor Susanne Woods, who made this all happen and took a chance on this crazy book idea I had!

To my photographer, Kristen Gardner, who helped make this book so beautiful. Your breathtaking images constantly make me gasp! To Peter Dahlquist for his ability to take an idea and sketch it so beautifully. Your illustrations are wonderful!

Of course, to Ruby, Alexa, and Molly, my little models, who braved subzero temperatures and still remained happy in every shot!

A mountain of love and thanks to each and every student at Little Pincushion Studio. You are the reason I do what I do, the reason I love what I do. You have given me so much joy in the creative journey we all take together.

Finally, thank you to my grandmother, Nin, whose crafting spirit I feel is with me in every stitch, every creative decision, and every great achievement. I miss you.

Contents

18 **Special Skills**
    Using patterns • Using fusible web
    • Hand sewing • Hot tools!

24 **Let's Talk Fabric**
    Cotton • Felt • Reuse and recycle

Projects

A note to parents from Heather Ross

The value of handmade objects, for most of us, is learned in childhood. It is in our nature to make things—a small but sure boat made from a leaf and stick, a first pretend pet imagined from a friendly looking pinecone and a few twigs, or even small but promising sculptures from our unloved mashed potatoes. As children, we will look at any object and instinctively ask ourselves how we might use or be amused by it. And with these exercises, we learn to create, to imagine, and to seek inspiration.

It seems crucial to our development, this process, and yet we hardly have to strain a brain cell anymore. As parents it is all too easy to provide quick, vivid entertainment in the form of technology. Of course we would rather give our children a simple bag of craft sticks and push them to imagine what fun could be had with them. But it's far too easy to hand them the iPad instead. Thank goodness for books like these, that put so much at our fingertips— gorgeous images, excellent how-to guidance, and most important of all, Promised Fun. Delivered.

Annabel Wrigley has done an exceptional job with this book, which should be included in every home and craft library. Annabel's crafts are designed to appeal to many ages. They are beautiful and in some cases quite useful. Her lovely, wistful photos will remind you that childhood is best spent out of doors surrounded by those you love—with enough paper, string, and glue to build a small city, and a bit of mud on your knees and elbows.

—Heather Ross

Heather Ross is an author and artist. Her illustrations appear on textiles and paper goods; on the pages of her books, *Weekend Sewing* and *Heather Ross Prints*; and on her blog, **heatherross.squarespace.com**.

7

Welcome!

I am so glad you decided to take the plunge and start sewing with me. Sewing is so much fun! Once you get the hang of it, you'll be amazed at the awesome things you can create all by yourself.

In my sewing classes at Little Pincushion Studio, I teach girls like you to sew. I love showing people how to make things! We make all sorts of fun projects just like the ones in this book.

I wrote this book because I really want to inspire you to start sewing. I want you to get creative and not be afraid to try something new. There are no complicated instructions. And perfection is optional! Listen—none of us is perfect. We all just try to be the best we can.

All the projects in this book have been designed just for you. Some of them may take a little bit more time than others. But I guarantee that all the work will be worth it in the end when you've created something that you are proud to call your own.

At the end of every sewing class I ask my girls, "What do you want to make next week?" This book is a collection of the most loved projects that we have made in class together. These are the projects that kids really do want to sew. I know you will, too.

Enjoy!

Annabel

How to use this book

In this book, you will find everything from cute owl stuffies to felt flower accessories. Some projects are pretty easy, and some are a bit more challenging. You'll notice that each project has a symbol at the top. Here's what each symbol means.

EASY PEASY

Start with these projects, especially if you are not super comfy yet with using your sewing machine. These are fun hand sewing projects that you'll have no trouble finishing.

easy peasy

A TEENY BIT MORE CHALLENGING

You'll need a little confidence for these projects. You should be comfortable with using the sewing machine and with hand sewing. You are going to have so much fun with these!

teeny bit challenging

TAKE YOUR TIME AND ASK FOR HELP

These projects need some patience and a great attitude. If you really know your way around your sewing machine, go for it! I know you can do it. You may want to ask for help from an adult or other experienced sewer. We all need a little help sometimes!

take your time, ask for help

I really think that working through the skill levels in the book will help you gain confidence. And you'll soon have the super crafty skills to tackle the challenging projects!

Thoughts to sew by

Gosh, I'll bet you are itching to dive in and get started on some of these projects!

Before you do, take just a minute to think about these important things.

1 Stay positive

Always start a project with a positive outlook. Some projects might look hard to make. But they're not! If you get stuck, take a break. Get a cookie and a glass of milk. Dance to your favorite song. Then come back and try again. You'll be amazed at how much better you'll feel.

2 Use your imagination

Please don't be afraid to be creative. Go ahead and mix some crazy fabrics together. Mix spots and stripes, florals and zigzags. These projects are all about you!

10

3 Practice, practice, practice

Successful sewing takes practice. I know you're excited to start! But take a little time to get comfortable with sewing first. Try out some hand stitches on fabric scraps. Sew some practice seams on your sewing machine. Make sure you're comfortable sewing straight lines. You'll be glad you did!

4 Sew like a snail

You may think that if you speed-sew, you will get your project finished faster. But really, you will end up making tons of mistakes. I want you to sew like a snail. Snails are really slow. But they do eventually get to where they need to be, right?

Make it your own 5

No two of us are the same. So why should our projects all look the same? You don't have to try to be perfect. Your project doesn't have to look just like the one in this book. Just express yourself. (You know you want to!) Remember, this is your project. Make it your own!

What Do I Need?

You can't sew without the proper supplies! Let's talk about all the bits and pieces you need to get started.

SEWING MACHINE AND EXTRA NEEDLES	It doesn't have to be a fancy machine. Read more about sewing machines in Your Sewing Machine (page 16).
1. PINS	Straight pearl-head pins are my faves.
2. HAND SEWING NEEDLES	General sharp hand sewing needles are fine.
3. SCISSORS	I have one pair for fabric and one pair for paper.
4. SEAM RIPPER	We all make mistakes! This handy little tool will help you rip out stitching that needs to be done over.
5. THREAD	This is regular all-purpose polyester sewing thread. I tend to use mainly white or black.
6. BUTTON THREAD	This poly/cotton thread is super strong. Use it to sew on buttons, of course. And it's useful when you are hand sewing through lots of layers of felt or fabric.
7. DISAPPEARING-INK FABRIC MARKER	Use these to mark things like stitching lines on fabric. When the project is finished, spray with a little water. The marks will just disappear! The Dritz Disappearing Ink Marking Pen in purple is my favorite.
8. RULER	I like the big, clear plastic quilter's rulers. The 6½″ × 24″ size is good. They're so easy to use!
9. MEASURING TAPE	Use this flexible "ruler" to measure your waist for a skirt, or for projects that don't lie flat.

Your Workspace

Okay, I find that to get in the sewing groove, I need to be set up in a nice, cozy spot. A great place may be your dining table. Or you could find a quiet little nook somewhere in your home. Maybe there is a little corner in the basement, or a cozy spot under the stairs.

- Keep your space tidy!

- Make sure you are sitting on a comfy chair that supports your back. Set your sewing machine on a solid, flat surface such as a table.

- Make sure your space is well lit. Have a good overhead light. If you are in a little nook somewhere, a good bright table lamp will work just fine. Don't forget to check that your sewing machine light is working well!

- Save snack time for when you have a break at the end of your project. Cookie crumbs sure do have a way of getting all over fabric! They get into the nooks and crannies on your sewing machine, too.

- Make sure you have all your supplies handy. Have a few little baskets for organizing your stuff. Why not make a few Happiness Storage Trays (page 96)? They'll make it easy to find what you need *and* to tidy up!

- Some fun background music might help you get in a crafty mood … give it a try!

Make sure you have all your supplies handy.

Basic Sewing Supplies

4. SEAM RIPPER

6. BUTTON THREAD

5. THREAD

3. SCISSORS

8. RULER

2. HAND SEWING NEEDLES

7. DISAPPEARING-INK FABRIC MARKER

9. MEASURING TAPE

1. PINS

ASSORTED TRIMS

BUTTONS

FUN STUFF!

BEADS

FABRIC AND FELT

EMBROIDERY FLOSS

15

Your sewing machine

Sewing on a machine is fun! If you are just starting out using your machine, carefully read the instruction book that came with it. Most manuals show you in words and pictures how to do things like thread the machine. They are pretty easy to understand. But if you get stuck, ask an adult to help you.

Sewing on a machine is fun!

Can't find the instruction book? You can usually find the instructions for your machine online. Hooray for the Internet!

THREADING THE MACHINE

Learn to thread your machine correctly. You'll need to thread both the needle and the bobbin. Most sewing machines are threaded in a similar way (unless you have a super-old one). Thread it in this order:

Spool pin → Thread guide → Thread take-up lever
Needle ← Thread guide ←

Remember, the machine will not sew properly if you miss even one little threading spot when threading the needle. So check and double-check before you start sewing. Wind the bobbin from the bobbin winder spindle. Be sure to thread the bobbin into the bobbin case and insert it into the machine correctly.

SEWING MACHINE NEEDLES

Always make sure you have a full packet of sewing machine needles on hand. If you sew a lot with felt, you may need to change your needle often. If a little screw holds the needle in place, unscrew it to pull out the old needle. Sometimes you can just unscrew it with your fingers. Your machine may have come with a little screwdriver. Always screw in the new needle nice and tight so it won't fall out.

THE PARTS OF YOUR MACHINE

Take a look at the drawing of a typical simple sewing machine. The main parts are labeled. You know what some parts like the needle do. Read on to learn about some of the parts that may be less familiar to you. Some parts may be in a different location on your machine. Check your manual if you cannot find all the listed parts on your machine.

Handwheel This lets you raise and lower the needle by hand. Always turn it toward you!

Tension control This controls the tension of the top thread. The tension of the thread is the tightness of the thread as it sews. If you get "nests" of thread or loose stitches when you sew, the tension needs adjusting. Ask an adult for help!

It is really important to have the top thread and the bobbin thread the same tightness. That will make your stitches look tip-top!

Thread take-up lever This helps maintain the thread tension as you sew.

Stitch width selector This controls the width of a zigzag stitch. Be sure yours is set to 0. That's a straight stitch, which is the one we'll be using in all the projects.

Feet Your sewing machine probably came with lots of different sewing feet. We are going to use only a regular foot. Exception: If you make the Zippy Pouch (page 86), you will need a zipper foot. Note: The sewing foot is also called a presser foot in your machine's manual.

Feed dogs These move the fabric evenly under the presser foot as you sew.

On/Off

Stitch length selector This controls the length of each stitch your machine makes. The smaller the stitch length, the stronger your stitching will be. Set your stitch length at about 2.5. This stitch is not so small that you need a magnifying glass to unpick any mistakes! If you have an older machine, you may have a dial that is a little different. The best thing to do is to set it to 12 ... that's about the same as 2.5.

Bobbin case

Bobbin

Foot control pedal

Special Skills

Using patterns

Many of the projects in this book have patterns for you to use. The pattern pieces are at the back of the book.

You will need to enlarge some of the patterns on a photocopier. The percentage to enlarge is on the pattern. Ask an adult to help you if you are not sure how to do this. Other patterns are just the right size in the book, so the best way to copy these pattern pieces is to trace them onto parchment paper. Or you could also copy the patterns using a photocopier.

Parchment paper makes the best tracing paper. It's a white paper on a roll. You can find it in the baking section of the supermarket. How easy is that?

FIND IT!

Look for parchment paper in the same section as aluminum foil in your local supermarket.

You can use these same instructions to trace a pattern onto fusible web.

TO USE A PATTERN, FOLLOW THESE STEPS.

1. Lay the parchment paper over the pattern. Use a pencil to trace carefully on the lines. If you have trouble seeing through the paper, you can put it up to a window or on a glass-topped table.

2. With paper scissors, cut out the shape on the lines.

3. Lay the paper pattern piece on your fabric. Pin it in place.

4. If you want to, you can draw around the pattern with a pencil. Then remove the pattern.

5. With fabric scissors, carefully cut out around the pattern or on the pencil lines. Take out the pins.

Using fusible web

You will use this iron-on material for lots of the projects in this book. You iron it onto the back of one fabric shape that you want to stick to another piece of fabric. I use double-sided fusible web. My favorite kind is HeatnBond Lite Iron-On Adhesive. You can find it at fabric stores. Before you use it, make sure to read the instructions on the package.

This web has paper on one side, the other side is slightly rough. Here's how to use it. The photos show steps from the Cross-Body Handy Pouch (page 62). This bag has an apple decoration made of felt.

Fusible web comes in packages and by the yard. Look for it at your local fabric store. Buy the lightweight type.

WEB GOO ALERT!

Sometimes you see a bunch of sticky goop collecting on the machine needle when you are sewing a lot of fusible web. Stop for a minute, and use your fingers to wipe it off before restarting.

TO USE FUSIBLE WEB, FOLLOW THESE STEPS.

When you iron fusible web, always make sure to turn off the steam and use a dry iron!

1. Trace the shape onto the paper side of the fusible web.

2. Iron the web to the felt with the rough side of the web down. After it's cool, cut out the shape.

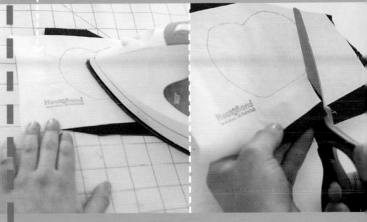

3. Peel off the paper. Position the shape where you want it on your fabric, fusible side down. Then iron it down. Now you can sew the edges of the shape to tack it down permanently.

Hand sewing

Okay, let's clear this up once and for all. Hand sewing is awesome and fun! And once you get the hang of it, it's pretty relaxing. I know it seems like more fun to let your sewing machine do all the work. But if you want to be a true sewing legend, learn how to hand stitch!

STITCHES

Before you sew, thread your needle and make a knot in the end of the thread.

Running stitch is the most basic hand sewing stitch. It's an up-and-down stitch. Knot your thread at the end. Poke the needle up from underneath the fabric, and pull the thread through to the top. Then poke the needle back down ¼" away. Pull the thread through to the back of the fabric again. Repeat this all along the seam. Keep your stitches even and neat. This is a good stitch to use when crafting with felt.

Whipstitch is for closing up openings in things like pillows or softies. Tie a knot in the end of your thread. Bring the needle up through one side and over the edge of the fabric. Then move a little to the side and down into the fabric. Try your hardest to keep your stitches small and even. Always make sure to tie a knot at the end.

SEWING ON A BUTTON

HERE'S WHAT TO DO WITH A TWO-HOLE BUTTON.

1. Mark the button spot on the project. Thread your needle with button thread.

Buttons can add so much to a project's look! You can sometimes find a jar of wonderful buttons in a thrift shop. Or you can cut buttons from thrift shop clothes. I bet if you look around your house or ask your parents, you'll find a few stray buttons hanging around.

Sewing on a button may look a little tricky, but it's actually super easy. Practice sewing one on a scrap of fabric before you add one to a "real" project. Some buttons have two holes and some have four.

2. Tie a knot in the end of the thread. Leave a long tail of thread.

3. Put the button on the fabric. Hold it down with your thumb. Bring the needle up from underneath the fabric. Poke it through one of the button's holes. Be sure to pull it all the way through.

4. Push the needle down through the other hole and out the back of the fabric.

5. Repeat Steps 3 and 4. Do them 2 or 3 times until the button feels nice and secure.

6. Bring the needle up from underneath the fabric, but don't go through the hole.

7. Wrap the thread around underneath the button several times.

8. Bring your needle back down to the underside of the fabric. Tie a knot with the beginning long thread tail, and trim off the extra threads.

21

Hot tools!

WATCH OUT!

Be super careful when you are using a tool that gets hot. Make sure you tell an adult that you are using it, and ask for help if you need it. The last thing we want to happen is for you to hurt yourself!

USING A HOT GLUE GUN

Electric hot glue guns are an amazing invention! You add a stick of solid glue. The glue melts, and you squeeze it out through the gun's nozzle. This glue dries in just seconds! Lots of projects in this book use a hot glue gun. You can use it to stick pieces of felt or fabric together. You can even use it to make pom-pom jewelry.

Glue guns come in different heat levels. *Please use only a low-temperature glue gun!* This tool will get hot enough to do the job, but it won't give you a yucky burn if you accidently hot glue yourself!

Always lay out your pieces before you start. Hot glue dries fast, so you will want to work quickly.

USING AN IRON

Using an iron the right way is important. It can mean the difference between a lovely pressed piece of fabric and one with a huge hole in it! Here are a few tips.

- Keep your fingers away from the iron as you use it on the fabric!

- Pay attention to the type of fabric you are using. Cotton can usually take the heat. But some fabrics that contain synthetics can melt if your iron is too hot. Make sure the dial on the iron is set to the correct fabric setting, such as Cotton or Wool.

- Never leave the iron lying with the soleplate down on your fabric!

- Always turn off your iron when you are finished.

A GREAT TOOL! You may notice that lots of the project pictures in this book show ironing on a surface with grid lines. That's a June Tailor Press-Mate ironing pad. It fits on your ironing board. It's heatproof and has a 1˝ grid printed on it. Cool!

Sewing Terms

As you make the projects in this book, you will come across some sewing terms that may leave you scratching your head. Here's a little roundup of what I mean when I say …

BACKSTITCH   Backstitching helps secure the stitching line so your sewing doesn't come undone. Start sewing a seam, and sew a few stitches. Stop, and hold down the reverse button on your machine. Now sew a few stitches backward. Then let go of the reverse button and sew forward. At the end of the seam, backstitch again.

EDGE OF THE PRESSER FOOT ON THE EDGE OF THE FABRIC   Many sewing machines have a regular presser foot that is ⅜″ wide. For that reason, these projects use a ⅜″ seam allowance. You can simply sew every seam with the edge of the presser foot on the edge of the fabric. Easy!

LEAVE A TAIL   It's so annoying when the machine needle comes unthreaded! To prevent this, leave a tail (long end) of thread about 8″ long before you start to stitch. It will save you a big headache!

RIGHT SIDES TOGETHER   It's important to sew with right sides together. This means that you match up the sewing edges of two pieces with the patterned sides or pretty sides facing. That way your project will come out nice and neat, with no raw edges showing on the right side of the project.

SEAM   This is the line you have sewn to join one piece of fabric to another piece of fabric.

SEAM ALLOWANCE   This is the distance between the edge of the fabric and the stitching line. The seam allowance for most of the projects in this book is ⅜″. Usually you will sew with the edge of the presser foot right next to the edge of the fabric, but some feet are not the right width. Be sure to check. It also helps to put a piece of blue painter's tape with the edge right at ⅜″. The tape becomes your sewing guide. If you sew too close to the edge of the fabric, you can wind up with wobbly and holey edges. Yikes!

SEWING AROUND A CORNER   For some projects, such as bags and pillows, you have to sew around the sides of a square or rectangle. This means that you have to sew around a corner. Start at the top right side, and, beginning with a backstitch, stitch down to the bottom corner. Stop the machine with the needle down. If necessary, turn the handwheel to get the needle to go down. Raise the presser foot and turn your fabric to sew down to the next corner. Lower the presser foot and stitch to the next corner. Continue doing this until you are all done. Don't forget to backstitch at the end!

TOPSTITCH   This means sewing ⅛″–¼″ from the edge around the outside of a completed project. Topstitching gives your project a neat-looking finish. To help you stitch straight, you can mark the stitch line using a disappearing-ink fabric marker before sewing.

Let's Talk Fabric

Ooh, lovely! Now we get to talk about the best part—fabric! I adore beautiful, colorful fabrics, don't you? The fabrics and colors you choose are so important to the look and feel of your project. I really want you to get creative with your color and pattern choices. Stripes and polka dots can look totally awesome together!

Shop for fabrics in your local quilt shop or fabric store.

COTTON

Cotton is the fabric to use in most of these projects. I love to use quilting cotton, which is lightweight and easy to sew. There are so many amazingly cute prints to choose from. Decorator-weight cotton fabrics are also great. These are a little heavier than quilting cotton. They're usually used to cover furniture. But a decorator-weight cotton is perfect for projects that need to be a little sturdier, such as the Super-Secret Journal Cover (page 91) and the Silhouette Pillow (page 117).

FELT

Oh, felt, I love you so! Felt is really great for crafting and sewing. It's sturdy, and when you cut the edges, they don't fray. This means you never have to hem felt. So it's perfect for pieces with unusual shapes. It comes in a gazillion colors, and it makes the cutest softies in town. You can find felt made from wool or synthetic material, or a blend. Some is even made from recycled plastic bottles. Can you believe that? I love to use 100% wool felt. It's a teeny bit harder to find than synthetic-blend felt, but it's wonderful to work with.

REUSE AND RECYCLE

One of my favorite things to do is to look through the clothing racks in thrift shops. You can find some amazing things! When I look at the clothing, instead of seeing some ugly-shaped dress, I see a fabulous piece of fabric. I hunt for worn flannel shirts and bright vintage dresses, wool sweaters and old quilts. I always come home with a bulging bag of treasures just waiting to be pulled apart!

You can even go shopping in your own home. We all have boxes of old clothes. Have you ever looked at them and thought, "No way am I ever wearing this old thing again"? Now look again in a different way. Hmmm—that dress is a bad style but a super-fun fabric. Make sure nobody else at home wants it. Then get out your scissors and start cutting.

UPCYCLING OLD SWEATERS

You may notice that some projects in this book use felted sweaters. Basil and Midge (page 153) are made of soft, cushy felted sweaters. Summer is a wonderful time to go thrift shopping for sweaters. They are usually only a couple of dollars each, so you can build a little collection.

How to Felt a Sweater

Find an old wool sweater that nobody wants. Read the label to make sure it's 100% wool. A lot of sweaters are made with different percentages of fibers. Some may be mixed with wool … so don't be fooled! These sweaters will not felt no matter how many times you wash them. The only way to get your sweater to felt up like a dream is to look on the label for 100% wool. I bet your dad has some chunky wool sweaters in the back of the closet!

1. Throw the sweater in the washing machine with regular detergent. Set the water temperature to hot, and wash on a regular cycle. Then put the sweater in a hot dryer.

2. The sweater should now have shrunk up to be really small. The knit should be almost invisible, like fabric. If not, it may take a couple more washes to get it perfect for cutting. We don't want that sweater to unravel!

3. Cut the sweater apart along the seams into flat pieces. That way, you can get as much usable fabric out of it as possible. In our Basil and Midge project (page 153), we use the cuff of a sweater for the hat. Just think of all the great projects you can make from all the parts of a sweater.

4. Now you can treat the pieces as you would a piece of fabric, and cut out the parts for your chosen project.

USING OLD DRESSES

Look in thrift shops for adult shirts, skirts, and dresses. You would be amazed by how much fabric you can get from just one dress! Find a dress or skirt made of fabric with a fun and striking pattern. Be sure to look at the fabric content on the label. Try to stick with garments that are mainly cotton. Pass up any garment that smells bad and/or has stains.

After washing the dress or shirt, cut it up. Cut along the seams to get the most usable fabric out of it. Don't throw away shirt cuffs! Cuffs can be repurposed into super-cool bracelets. What a great way to recycle, right? You can also find beautiful buttons on some clothing. Save those, too.

Accessorize

Blooming Headband

what do I need?

- Piece of felt at least 4″ × 20″ in your favorite color for the flower
- Piece of green felt at least 5″ × 5″ for the leaves
- Plain headband
- Several seed beads
- Hot glue gun and gluestick
- Basic supplies (Refer to pages 12 and 14.)

special skills

- Using patterns (page 18)
- Hand sewing (page 20)
- Using a hot glue gun (page 22)

Prepare the pieces

Leaf and circle patterns are on page 166.

1. Cut a strip of felt 4″ × 18″ for a larger flower. Or cut it 3″ × 18″ for a slightly smaller flower.

2. Trace the circle pattern. Cut 1 circle out of the same color felt as your flower.

3. Trace the leaf pattern. Cut 2 leaves from green felt.

Let's make it!

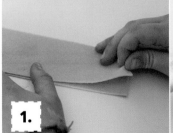

1.

Fold the strip of felt in half. Pin it to hold the fold in place.

2.

With scissors, cut even slits about ¼″ apart in the folded edge. Be careful so you stop cutting ¼″–½″ from the opposite edge. Cut slits along the entire strip.

Don't flowers just make you happy?
Imagine how happy you'll be when you're wearing a little bit of springtime happiness on your head!

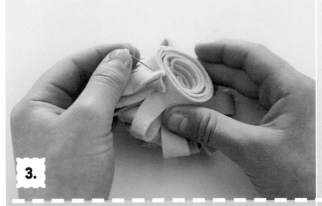

3.

Take out the pins, and very carefully roll up the strip as tightly as you can. Pin the end of the strip to hold it in place.

4.

Thread a needle with button thread and knot the end of the thread. Begin from the center, and push the needle through all the layers to the outside of the flower. Push the needle back through the center and then through the layers again to a point about ¼″ away from where you sewed it the first time. Keep sewing back through the center and then through the layers, moving around the circle with each stitch. As you sew, the thread will make a kind of star pattern holding everything together. Pull the thread nice and tight after each stitch.

GLUE IT!

You can do this part with hot glue. But sewing gives the flower the fullness it needs to look flowertastic!

5.

Finish by tying a knot in the thread.

6.

Use your fingers to fluff out the flower to the desired fabulousness.

7.

Add a dab of hot glue in the center of the flower.

8.

Drop in a couple of seed beads for extra va-va-voom.

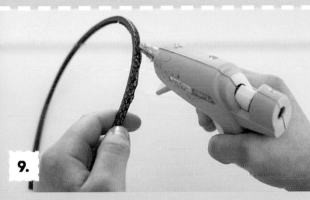

9.

Decide where the flower will be on the headband. Slightly to the side seems to look the best. With your hot glue gun, carefully run a bead of glue along the headband. Make it about the length of the leaf.

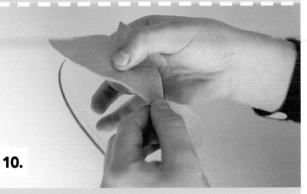

10.

Attach the leaf. Now do the same with the other leaf.

11.

Put a big dab of glue on both the flower and the felt circle.

12.

Carefully press the flower onto the headband, with the circle on the underside of the band. This will hold the flower and headband together nice and tight! Wait a few minutes for it to dry completely.

Spring Bling Rings

what do I need?

Makes 1 ring.

- Piece of felt at least 3″ × 9″ in your favorite color*

- Scrap of green felt at least 1½″ × 2½″ (for the daisy ring leaf)

- Ring blank (Find this in the jewelry-making section of a craft store.)

- Several tiny seed beads (Find these in the jewelry-making section of a craft store.)

- Hot glue gun and gluestick

- Basic supplies (Refer to pages 12 and 14.)

* You can also use a piece of felted sweater (page 26).

special skills

- Using patterns (page 18)

- Hand sewing (page 20)

- Using a hot glue gun (page 22)

CHOICE #1:
CHRYSANTHEMUM RING

Leaf pattern is on page 165.

Prepare the piece

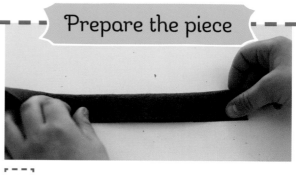

1. Cut a strip of felt 2″ × 5″.

2. Fold it in half along the length, and pin it to hold the fold in place.

Let's make it!

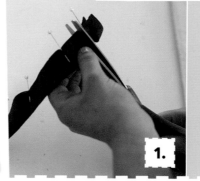

Cut slits in the folded edge. Be careful to stop ¼″–½″ from the open edge of the felt. The closer together you cut the slits, the fuller your flower will look.

1.

What can be sweeter than a spring garden on your finger? Hmmm ... the hardest part will be choosing which flower to make! I'll show you how to make a chrysanthemum and a daisy.

2.

Carefully roll up the strip nice and tight. Secure it with a pin.

3.

Thread a needle with a long piece of button thread. Start at the loose end of the felt. Push the needle through to the center and then back through the layers again to a point beside where you sewed it the first time. Keep sewing from the outside through the center, moving around the circle with each stitch. As you sew, the thread will make a kind of star pattern holding everything together. Pull the thread nice and tight after each stitch. When you get to the end, tie a knot.

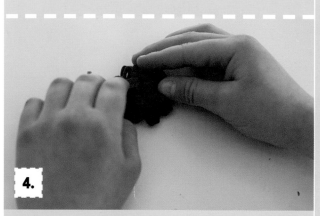

4.

Fluff out the petals so they look nice and full.

5.

Squeeze a big dab of hot glue on the top of your ring. Add the flower and hold it for a minute or 2 until it is super dry.

6.

Gently pull apart the flower to show the center. Squeeze a small dab of hot glue in the center. Drop in 3 or 4 little seed beads.

CHOICE #2:
DAISY RING

Leaf pattern is on page 165.

1. Trace the leaf pattern. Cut 1 from green felt.

2. Cut 1 strip of felt 1″ × 8″

Let's make it!

1.

Cut slits along one edge, stopping about ¼″ from the top.

2.

Roll up the strip, and secure it with a pin.

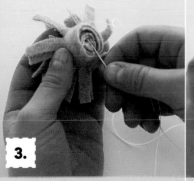

3.

Thread a needle with a long piece of button thread and knot the end. Start at the loose end of the rolled felt. Sew large stitches from the outside to the center. Work your way around the flower. When you get to the end, tie a knot.

4.

Add a dab of hot glue to the ring top. Attach the little leaf.

5.

Squeeze a big dab of hot glue on the bottom of your daisy. Press it down firmly on the ring. Hold it for a minute or 2 until it is super dry.

6.

Pull apart the petals to see the center. Add some hot glue and sprinkle in a couple of beads.

Spool Jewels

what do I need?

- Wooden spools (Check your grandma's sewing basket to see if she has any, or you can find these in the wood craft section of a craft store.)

- Scraps of yarn in fun colors

- Skeins of embroidery floss in fun colors

- Little beads (if you want to use them) (Make sure their holes are big enough for an embroidery needle to fit through.)

- Approximately 1 yard of something to hang your fabulous bling from—such as cord, chain, or a piece of leather

- Hot glue gun and gluestick

- Embroidery needle

- Basic supplies (Refer to pages 12 and 14.)

special skills

- Using a hot glue gun (page 22)

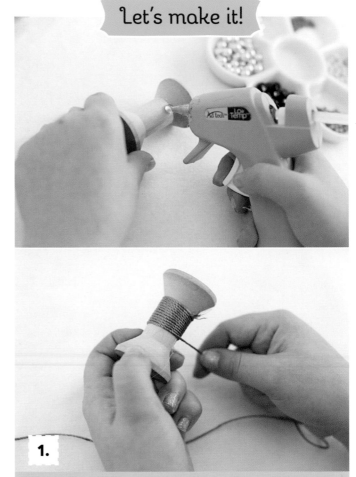

Let's make it!

1.

Put a drop of hot glue on your spool. Stick down the end of the piece of yarn, and start wrapping it tightly around the spool.

Who doesn't love to wear jewelry?
Bet you never thought you could turn an old spool into a fabulous jewel! Don't stop at just one. Make a whole necklace full of super-duper spool jewels!

2.

When you get to the end, add another drop of glue. Trim the yarn and stick it in place.

3.

Put another dab of glue just inside the spool hole. Attach the end of the embroidery floss.

4.

Thread your embroidery needle with embroidery floss. Bring the floss in and out of the hole. Arrange the floss around the spool however you choose.

5.

When you have finished, trim the thread and secure it with a dab of glue on the inside of the spool hole.

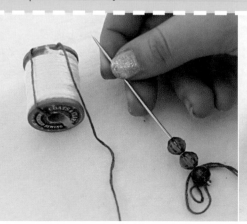

You could make one spool jewel look a little different by threading beads into the embroidery thread. How fun is that?

Now make a whole bunch of spool jewels in all different colors. You could use all different types of twine and yarn for a fun and fabulous look! Thread them onto your chain or cord, and tie the ends together. Done!

Blossoming Necklace

Finished length: About 48″

what do I need?

- ¼ yard of bright quilting cotton

- ¼ yard of plain or printed quilting cotton for the flowers

- Large bag of ½″ plastic craft beads

- Chopstick or knitting needle for turning your work

- Sewing machine

- Basic supplies (Refer to pages 12 and 14.)

special skills

- Using patterns (page 18)

- Hand sewing (page 20)

- Using an iron (page 22)

- Sewing around a corner (page 23)

Prepare the pieces

Flower pattern is on page 166.

1. Decide how many flowers you want. You will be making clusters of flowers. Each cluster works best with about 6 flowers. I like to use 4–6 clusters of flowers on a necklace. But it's really up to you.

2. Use the pattern to cut out all your flowers from the quilting cotton.

3. Cut 2 strips 3″ × the width of the fabric for the necklace.

This cute necklace makes me think of long, warm summer days. It's kind of like wearing a garden around your neck (without the bugs, of course!).

Let's make it!

1.

Fold a flower into fourths by folding it in half and then in half again. Iron it. Repeat for all the flowers. Set them aside.

2.

Sew the 2 strips of fabric together end to end to create a super-long strip. Measure the strip, and cut it at 60″.

3.

Fold the strip in half along its length, right sides together. Iron it along the fold. Pin all along the open side of the strip.

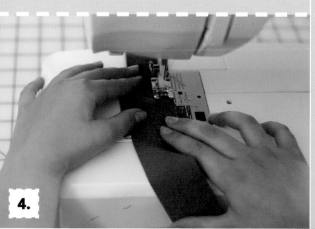

Carefully stitch along the open long side of the strip. Sew with the edge of the presser foot on the edge of the fabric.

4.

Thrift shops are a great place to find old bead necklaces just crying out to be cut up and repurposed. Isn't recycling awesome!

5.

When you reach the bottom, sew across the short end. Secure with a backstitch. You should have a long tube with one closed end.

6.

Now turn the tube right side out. This looks hard, but it's really not! The secret is a chopstick or knitting needle. Start at the sewn end. Use the chopstick to gently push the end inside itself. As you push the tube right side out, keep pulling down the edges.

7.

Use your measuring tape to measure 10˝ from the closed end of the tube. Tie a knot.

HOW LONG?

It's good to leave 10˝ of fabric at each end of your necklace. This way, you can adjust the length when you tie it around your neck.

8.

Feed a plastic bead down inside the tube to the knot. Now tie a knot in the tube right above the bead. Add a second bead, and tie a knot above it.

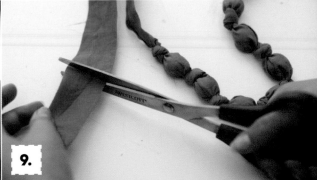

9.

Keep going until your necklace is the length you want. Tie the final knot. Measure about 10½˝, and cut off the end of the tube.

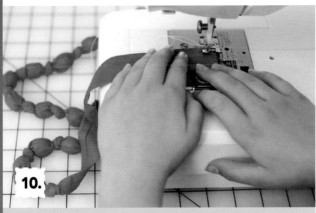

10.

Fold in ½" of the open end, and topstitch it closed.

11.

Thread a needle and knot the thread. Stack 6 folded flowers in your hand, with the folded corners on top of each other.

12.

Push the needle through the folded corners of all 6 flowers. Now push the needle through one of the knots between the beads. Push it though a second time.

13.

Tie a knot to secure the thread.

Add as many flower clusters as you want. Remember to tie the thread in a knot at the end of every cluster. That way the flowers won't fall off your necklace.

14.

You could always add some sweet little embellishments, such as butterflies and buttons, to make the necklace more "you." Either way, tie it around your neck, and prepare yourself for compliments!

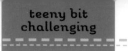

Folded Flower Pin

Finished size: About 3½″ across

what do I need?

Makes 1 flower.

- 8 small pieces of different printed cotton fabrics, each a little bigger than 4″ × 4″

  - Pretty button

  - Scrap of felt at least 2″ × 2″

  - Pin back (Find it in the jewelry-making section of a craft supply store.)

- Hot glue gun and gluestick

- Basic supplies (Refer to pages 12 and 14.)

special skills

- Using patterns (page 18)

- Hand sewing (page 20)

- Using an iron (page 22)

- Using a hot glue gun (page 22)

Prepare the pieces

Circle pattern is on page 165.

1. Use your ruler and scissors to cut 8 squares of fabric. Each should measure 4″ × 4″. These will be the flower petals.

2. Cut 1 felt circle using the pattern.

Let's make it!

1.

Fold each square in half to make a triangle. Iron.

For this project we will be using an **ancient Japanese fabric-folding technique known as** *kanzashi*. It sounds complicated, but as you'll see, it's easy and fun!

2.

Place 1 of the triangles with the fold at the bottom. Fold in each corner toward the open top point to make a diamond.

3.

Flip the diamond over sideways to the plain unfolded side. Be sure to keep it pointed in the same direction.

TIP

When you flip over the square, be sure to keep the center folds facing up and down. You have to flip it over sideways or it will not work. After you have flipped it, take a peek underneath to double check.

4.

Fold in each corner so the points meet in the middle.

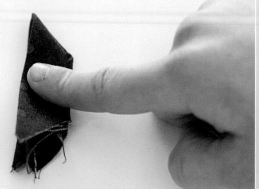

5.

Fold the piece of folded fabric in half. Slide a pin through the middle to hold it all in place. Set it aside.

6.

Repeat Steps 1–5 with your other 7 flower petals.

7.

The raw-edged points at the end will not be needed. Cut the end off in a straight line. Make sure you do this at the same place on each petal.

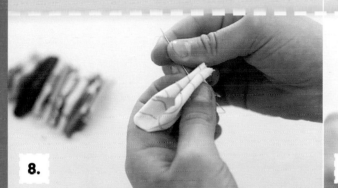

8.

Thread a needle with button thread. Push the needle through each petal at the same place close to the trimmed petal base. Thread it through all 8 petals. Do not pull the thread all the way through. Leave a long tail!

9.

When all the petals are on the thread, pull to make a circular flower shape. Tie the ends together. Don't tie it so tight that the petals are too smooshed. But don't tie it too loose, either. You'll know when it looks right.

10.

Arrange all the petals so that they are even.

11.

Push down on the center to open up each petal.

Folded Flower Pin

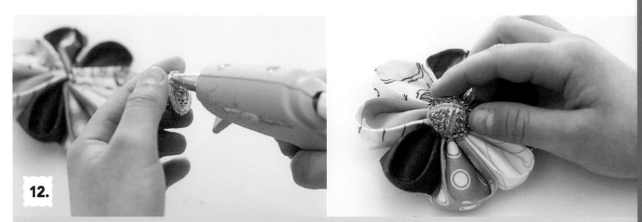

12.

Hot glue a button to the flower center.

13.

Hot glue the felt circle on the underside of the flower. Attach the pin back with hot glue.

Folding is soooo much fun!

Five-Minute Fancies

Pom-Poms

what do I need?

- 1 ball of lovely yarn
- A hand (preferably your own!)
- Scissors

Let's make it!

1.
Hold the end of the yarn between your fingers. Start wrapping it around the widest part of your palm. Don't wrap it too tightly or the pom-pom will come out too small—and your hand may turn blue!

2.
Wrap about 50 times. (You may need to wrap thinner yarn 70 times.) Cut the yarn from the ball. Carefully pull the bundle off your hand. Keep it all together!

3.
Cut a piece of yarn a few inches long, and tie it tightly around the center of the yarn bunch. Make a good knot so it holds.

4.
Using a sharp pair of scissors, cut through all the loops.

5.
Time to make the pom-pom look lovely and round! Fluff out the yarn and use your scissors to give the pom-pom a little haircut.

Who doesn't love pom-poms? String them on a garland, or hang them on a bag or a lamp pull. Or make them just because they are too cute for words. I haven't met a girl who didn't want to learn how to make a pom-pom. **So easy!**

Button Ring

what do I need?

Makes 1 ring.

- Buttons (1 small, 1 medium, 1 larger)
- Ring blank (Find this in the jewelry-making section of a craft supply store.)
- Hot glue gun and gluestick

special skills

- Using a hot glue gun (page 22)

Let's make it!

1.

Put a dab of hot glue on the back of the medium button. Center it on top of the large button, and press firmly. Then glue the small button on top of that.

How about a little button bling?

Get creative with buttons. Stack them, bedazzle them—the choice is yours. You will be sure to have the most stylish fingers on the block!

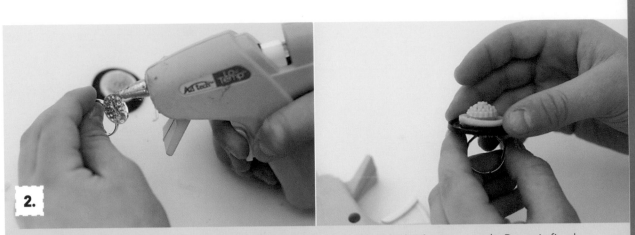

2.

Place a big dab of hot glue on the top of your ring blank. Attach the button stack. Press it firmly to make sure it is stuck down really well.

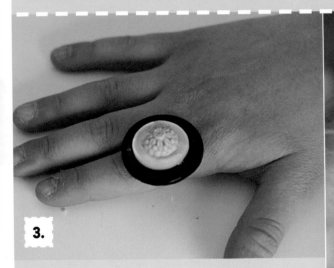

3.

Wait a few minutes before wearing your ring. You want the glue to be set and super dry.

Don't stop with a ring. You can also use this idea to make the cutest barrettes in town!

Fabulous Felt Barrette

We love all things **geometric!** How about making your own little piece of wearable geometric art?

what do I need?

- Small felt scraps in 3 different colors
- Long flat-top barrette (Find it at a craft supply store.)
- Hot glue gun and gluestick

special skills

- Using patterns (page 18)
- Using a hot glue gun (page 22)

Let's make it!

Triangle patterns are on page 171.

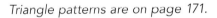

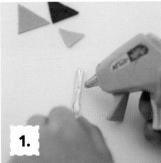

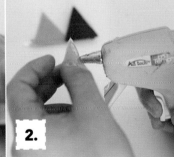

1. Trace the patterns, and cut 1 smaller and 2 larger triangles from the felt. Run a line of hot glue along the top of the barrette.

2. Glue the 2 large triangles side by side. Put a dab of glue on the back of the small triangle. Attach it between the other triangles.

Pom-Pom Earrings

These **seriously cute pom-tastic earrings** will have you feeling warm and fuzzy all over!

what do I need?

Makes 1 pair.

- 2 tiny matching pom-poms or small felted balls (Find these in all sizes at a craft or hobby store.)

- Earring post findings (Find these in the jewelry-making section of a craft supply store.)

- Hot glue gun and gluestick

----> special skills

- Using a hot glue gun (page 22)

Let's make it!

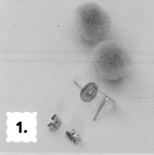

1.

Take off the earring backs, and lay out the pieces.

2.

Put a dab of glue on the cup of the earring piece. Add the pom-pom, and hold it in place for a minute or 2. Repeat with the other earring.

Not Your Grandma's Doily Tank

what do I need?

- Plain colored tank top

- Crocheted doily (Find it in a craft store or thrift shop.)

- Fabric dye (I use Rit dye from the supermarket.)

- Double-sided fusible web (measuring a little larger than the doily) (Refer to Using Fusible Web, page 19.)

- Apron or old clothes

- Rubber gloves

- Wooden spoon

- Old plastic dishpan

- Measuring cup

- Sewing machine

- Basic supplies (Refer to pages 12 and 14.)

special skills

- Using fusible web (page 19)

- Using an iron (page 22)

Dyeing the doily

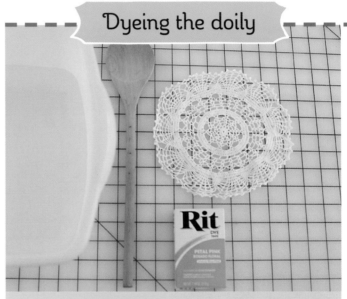

You can dye your doily in a color to match the tank top. Or choose any color you like. First, put on your apron or old clothes, please! And ask an adult for setup and dyeing help.

MAKE EXTRAS!

As long as you are mixing dye, you might want to dye several doilies. Then you'll have some ready for making more tops!

TURN PAGE for more doily dyeing ⟶

How adorable is this tank top with that **hand-dyed doily gorgeousness?** This is such an easy and fun project. You'll have to make one for each of your friends!

1. Rinse the doily in cold water and set it aside.

2. Read the instructions on the dye package. Measure out water, and put it in the dishpan. Add the dye, and stir it in until all the little dye crystals have dissolved. To keep your hands from getting dyed too, wear rubber gloves.

3. Dunk the doily in the dye. Leave it in for the amount of time stated on the package. Don't scrunch up the doily in the dye—try to flatten it out so it dyes evenly. For a lighter color, leave it in for a shorter time. A dyed piece is always darker when wet than when it dries, so leave it until it is a little darker than you want it.

4. Take the doily out of the dye. Rinse it well in cold running water. Make sure you rinse until the water runs clear! Set it aside to dry.

Let's make it!

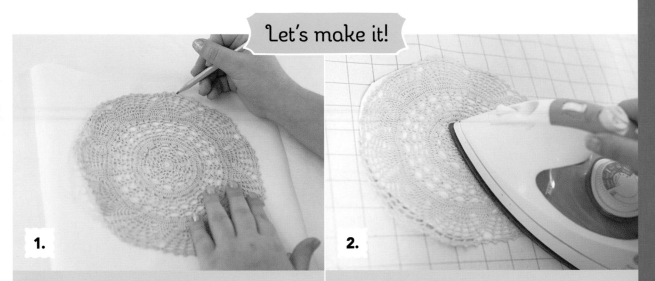

1. Place the dry doily on the paper side of the fusible web. Trace around the doily.

2. Cut out the circle. Position the circle of fusible web with the rough side facing up, and iron the doily onto the circle.

3.

Peel off the backing paper.

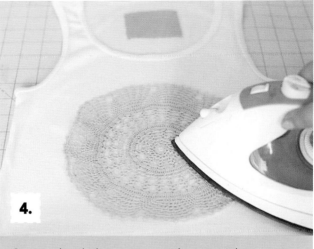

4.

Center the doily on your tank top, sticky side down, and iron.

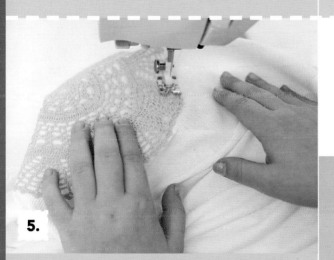

5.

Now we'll sew the doily to the tank top. Carefully slide the tank top under your sewing machine presser foot. Make sure that only the tank front is under the foot. You don't want to sew the front and back together! Line up the edge of the doily with the edge of the foot. You'll find that the doily is a little bit lumpy and bumpy. Sew slowly, and just do your best to sew evenly. When you're done, trim all the threads.

MAKE IT YOURS!

I like the look of the centered doily. But you can iron it on anywhere you want. You could even add more than one doily to your tank top. Remember, this is your project!

Marvel at the gorgeous tank top you just created. It's one of a kind!

Cross-Body Handy Pouch

Finished size: 9½˝ × 11½˝   **Fabrics:** Anna Maria Horner • Kokka

what do I need?

- ½ yard of fun printed fabric for the outer bag

- ½ yard of heavier cotton for the lining

- ¼ yard of fabric for the strap

- Scraps of felt in several colors for the bag decoration (Felt scraps for the large apple and mushroom pieces need to be at least 4˝ × 5˝.)

- ¼ yard or large scrap of double-sided fusible web

- ⅓ yard of featherweight fusible interfacing* (I use Pellon Fusible Featherweight.)

- Sewing machine

- Basic supplies (Refer to pages 12 and 14.)

* Interfacing is a material that you iron onto your fabric to make it a little stiffer. Find it at fabric and quilt stores.

special skills

- Using patterns (page 18)
- Using an iron (page 22)
- Using fusible web (page 19)
- Sewing around a corner (page 23)

Prepare the pieces

Apple and mushroom patterns are on pages 166, 167, and 171.

1. Decide whether you want an apple or a mushroom for your bag decoration. Trace the pattern pieces of your choice onto the paper side of the fusible web.

2. With the paper side up, iron the fusible web pieces to the felt colors of your choice. Cut out the pieces.

MAKE IT YOURS!

You can create your own design for a decoration. Draw it on the paper side of the fusible web. Then follow the directions just as for the apple or mushroom. Remember, your design will be the reverse of what you draw, so take care if you are adding a design with letters or numbers.

You will be the coolest gal in town with this adorable bag. Add a cute apple or mushroom decoration. And go ahead—personalize it. Hang a tassel or two off the strap!

3. Cut 2 pieces of printed fabric 10″ × 12″ for the outside of the bag.

4. Cut 2 pieces of heavier fabric 10″ × 12″ for the lining.

5. Cut 2 pieces of featherweight fusible interfacing 10″ × 12″.

6. Cut 2 pieces of fabric 4″ × 24″ for the straps.

7. Read the package directions for the fusible interfacing. Lay 1 piece of the interfacing on the wrong side of 1 outside bag piece. The rough side of the interfacing should face the wrong side of the fabric. Iron the 2 pieces together. Make sure they are stuck nice and tight. You may need to iron back and forth a bit. Repeat with the other outside bag and interfacing pieces.

Let's make it!

This bag has an outside, a lining, and a strap.
Just work slowly and make one part at a time.
Sew as slow as a snail and as straight as you can.
This is really good straight-sewing practice!

OUTSIDE BAG

1.

THINK AHEAD!

Make sure the felt shape is not positioned too close to the edge. Otherwise, it could get caught in the seam allowance when you stitch the bag together.

Also, make sure you have the decoration exactly where you want it. Once you've ironed down the pieces, you can't move them!

Peel off the backing paper, and position your felt decoration pieces in the lower corner of the front outside bag piece.

2.

Iron down the decoration.

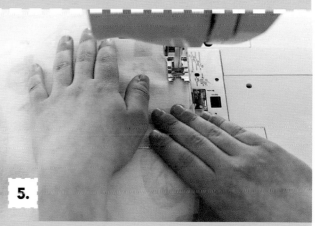

3.

Sew around the edges of the felt decoration to hold it in place. Stitch nice and close to the edge of the fabric. Try your hardest to keep your stitching even.

4.

Let's put the bag together. Place the bag outside pieces right sides together. Pin around the sides and bottom. Leave the top open.

5.

Sew the pieces together. Sew with the edge of the presser foot on the edge of the fabric. Start at the top right corner. Sew down to the bottom, across the bottom, and up the other side. Don't forget to backstitch at the beginning and end! Turn the bag right side out.

LINING

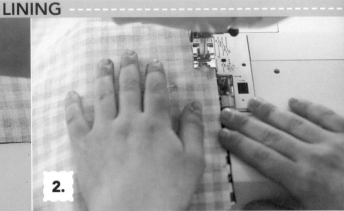

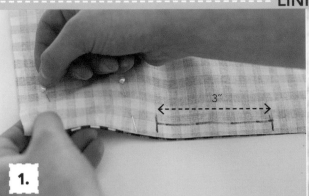

1.

Place the lining front and back with right sides together. Measure a 3″ space in the center of the bottom edge. Use a disappearing-ink marker to mark a 3″ line. When you sew you will leave this 3″ unsewn so you can turn the bag right side out through the hole.

2.

Sew the pieces together. Sew with the edge of the presser foot on the edge of the fabric. Start at the top right corner, and sew down to the bottom corner. Stop and turn. Sew across the bottom, but stop at the beginning of your marked 3″ line. Backstitch. Then start sewing again at the end of the marked line. Sew across the rest of the bottom and up the other side. Backstitch at every stop and start.

STRAP

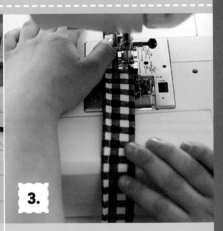

1.

Fold the 24″ strip in half, wrong sides together, and iron it. Now, using the center crease as a guide, fold in each long edge so they meet in the middle. Do the same with the other handle.

2.

Now fold the strips in half along their length. Iron them nice and flat.

3.

Topstitch down both edges of each strap. Sew nice and close to the edge.

1.

Pin one end of each strap to the outside bag, centered on a side seam of the bag. (Look carefully at the picture.) Line up the ends with the bag top, and pin.

2.

With the lining still inside out, gently push the outside bag into the lining. Keep the strap facing down toward the bottom, out of the way. Line up the tops of the inside and outside bags. Pin all the way around. Before you start sewing, make sure that the straps are pushed down into the bag and not all bunched up in there.

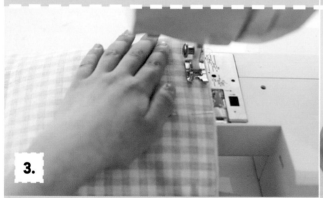

3.

You may need to take the extension table off your machine if you have one. This makes it easier to sew around the top in a kind of circle. Sew all the way around with the edge of the presser foot on the edge of the fabric, and remove the pins.

4.

Remember the 3″ gap you left in the lining bottom? Carefully pull the bag right side out through that hole.

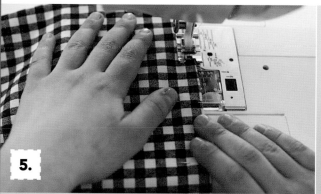

5. Fold in the edges of the hole you left in the lining piece. Iron. Topstitch the hole closed. Sew close to the edge!

6. Push the lining down into the bag. Make sure to push out the corners well.

7. Yay! Now you just need to iron around the top.

8. Now tie the handle ends together in a knot. You can tie the knot high or low. It all depends on how long or short you want your bag handles to be!

Cross-Body Handy Pouch

Flower Power Tee

what do I need?

- Plain T-shirt
- ¼ yard of printed quilting cotton
- Basic supplies (Refer to pages 12 and 14.)

special skills

- Using patterns (page 18)
- Hand sewing (page 20)
- Using an iron (page 22)

Prepare the pieces

Flower pattern is on page 166.

You can make as many or as few flowers as you want. They will go together in bunches of 4.

1. Trace the flower pattern. Pin the pattern on your fabric, and draw around it.

2. Draw and cut out as many flowers as you can from your piece of fabric. If you layer the fabric, you can cut several flowers at the same time.

Let's make it!

1. & 2.

Fold 1 flower in half and then in half again into fourths. Iron it. Repeat for all the flowers. Set them aside.

Thread your needle with button thread. Tie a knot in the end, but leave a 3″ tail beyond the knot.

Channel your inner flower child in this cute-as-can-be T-shirt decked with flowers. **You can add as many flower clusters as you want!**

Flower Power Tee

3.

MAKE IT PRETTY!

Place the bunches of flowers close together. It will give your T-shirt a really nice, ruffly look!

Decide where on your T-shirt you want the first bunch of flowers. Mark the place with a pin. To make a bunch, hold 4 of the folded flowers together at the folded points.

4.

5.

Push your needle through the T-shirt from behind. Push it through the folded corners of the 4 flowers. Bring the needle back down through the T-shirt, and pull the thread so the points are tight to the shirt. Repeat this up-and-down stitch 2 more times.

Tie a double knot with the button thread and button thread tail, and trim. Fluff out the flowers.

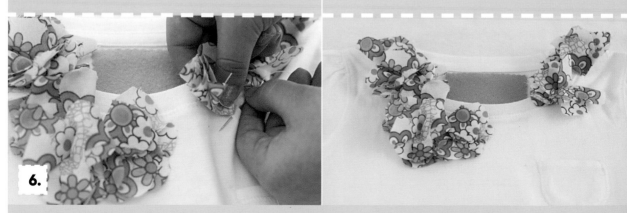

6.

Continue adding bunches of flowers until you have created a look you love!

Super-Simple Skirt

Fabrics: Clothfabric (Australia)

what do I need?

- Printed quilting cotton fabric (The amount of fabric will depend on your measurements. See Steps 1 and 2, page 75, to figure this out.)

- 1 yard of 2″-wide knitted elastic (I like black, but you can use any color.)

- Sewing machine

- Basic supplies (Refer to pages 12 and 14.)

special skills

- Using an iron (page 22)

Prepare the pieces

Wash your cotton fabric in warm water. Dry it in the dryer. If it's going to shrink, you want that to happen before you start cutting and sewing. That way, your wonderful skirt will still fit you no matter how many times you wash it!

MEASURE FIRST!

Don't buy any fabric until you have checked your measurements! You may need more fabric if your waist measurement (doubled) is larger than the width of the fabric. Read the steps for measuring.

What's more fun than a skirt you made yourself? It's pretty hard to stop at just one. Let your inner fashion designer take this basic pattern and make it your own. Add some pom-poms or stitch on some trim. You could even add a pocket.

1. Take your measurements with a measuring tape. This is easiest with a partner. Measure your waist at the point where the waistband will sit. Make sure it's not too low on your hips. Write down your measurement on paper.

2. Take 2 times your waist measurement to get the amount of fabric you need to buy. For example, if your waist measures 24″, you will buy 48″ of fabric. (You can't buy exactly 48″ of fabric, but you can buy 1⅜ yards, which is 49½″ of fabric—close enough.) No more cutting is needed for the width of the skirt, except to straighten the ends of the fabric.

3. Measure how long you would like your skirt to be. This skirt looks best a little above the knee. Make a note of that measurement.

4. Add 2″ to your skirt length measurement from Step 3. Measure and cut your skirt fabric to this length. When you measure the fabric, make sure that you have the selvage running down the side or length of your fabric piece. Make sure to cut as straight as you can. I usually use a ruler and a disappearing-ink marker for this part!

5. Subtract 2″ from your waist measurement from Step 1. Measure and cut the elastic to this length.

LEFTOVER FABRIC

You will have a long strip of leftover fabric after you cut out your skirt. Use it to make another project—such as a matching Blossoming Necklace (page 39), a Cross-Body Handy Pouch (page 62), or a cute Super-Secret Journal Cover (page 91). You could even make a little something for your BFF. It's fun to be creative with fabric leftovers!

1.

MARK THE SPOT

You can make it super easy to sew a 1˝ seam. Measure 1˝ to the right from your sewing machine needle. Stick down a small piece of blue painter's tape. Use this as a guide. Then just pull off the tape when you're finished.

Fold the elastic in half, and line up the 2 raw ends. Sew the ends together with a 1˝ seam allowance.

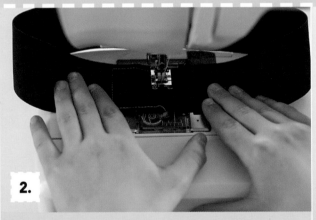

2.

3.

Open out and flatten the ends of the elastic. Sew around the opened-out edges in a square. (Look at the picture for Step 5 below to see the finished square.)

Fold your skirt piece in half with right sides together. Carefully match up the edges. Pin it down the length of the fabric.

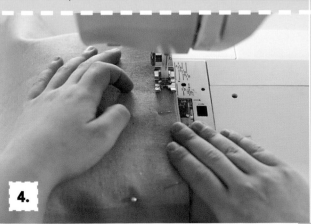

4.

Sew down the side, with the edge of the presser foot on the edge of the fabric. When you are done, iron down the seam you have just sewn, just to make it lovely and flat.

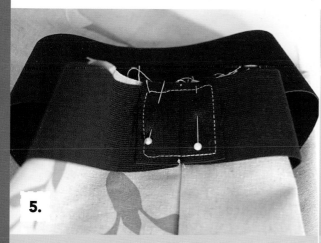

5.

Now attach the elastic. Turn the skirt right side out. Line up the elastic seam with the skirt seam. Line up the edge of the elastic with the raw edge around the skirt top.

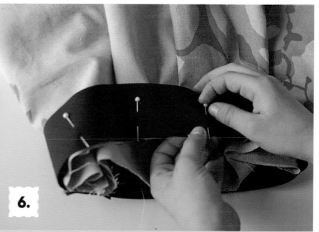

6.

Divide your skirt into sections. Start by dividing it into fourths and then again into eighths, and mark the spots with pins. Now do the same with the elastic. Now all you need to do is line up the pins, and pin the elastic to the skirt at those points. This helps keep the elastic evenly in place around the skirt.

7.

TIP

If you have a sewing machine with a button that makes the needle end in the down position when you stop sewing, now would be the time to press that button. If your machine doesn't have it, make sure that every time you stop the sewing machine, the needle is down in the fabric.

There's a little trick to sewing elastic. Sew with the edge of the presser foot on the edge of the elastic. Hold on to the elastic and fabric from behind the presser foot with your left hand. At the same time, hold the elastic and fabric in front with your right hand, and pull it taut as you sew. This helps everything stay flat instead of bunching up. Finish with a backstitch.

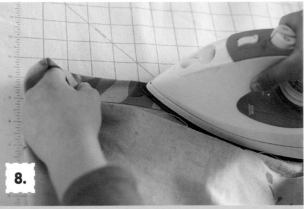

8.

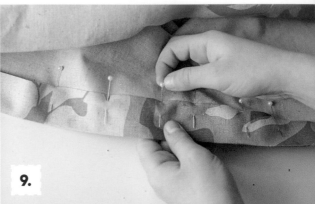

9.

Now you're ready to hem your skirt. Try it on, just to be sure that it will be the right length with a 2˝ hem. To create the hem, fold up the bottom 1˝. Iron it flat. Then fold up the hem 1˝, and iron it again.

Pin the hem in place.

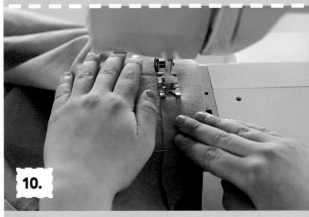

10.

With the edge of the presser foot on the edge of the folded fabric, sew as straight as you can all the way around the hem. Remember to back-stitch. When you are done, trim your threads.

Turn your skirt right side out.

Hooray—you're finished!
Be sure to tell everyone
that you made it!

DIY FABRIC DESIGN

Why not be creative and print your own fabric? You could tie-dye a piece of cloth, draw a design with fabric markers—the options are endless. Here I'll show you how to stencil on fabric. This project uses a ready-made bag. But you can do the same thing on a piece of fabric. Then sew it up into anything that tickles your fancy!

You will need freezer paper to make your stencil. You can find it at any grocery store, or you can get sheets of it from C&T Publishing. Freezer paper has a shiny, waxy side that can be stuck temporarily to fabric using an iron.

what do I need?

Heart pattern is on page 172.

- Fabric paints (I like DecoArt SoSoft Fabric Acrylics.)
- Paint tray, old plate, or even a paper plate
- Plain canvas tote bag
- Freezer paper
- Craft knife
- Self-healing cutting mat
- Stencil brush (You can either use one with bristles, or you can use one with a sponge on the end.)
- Pencil

Let's make it!

Cut a piece of freezer paper the size of the print area you need. Draw your design on the nonshiny side. Leave plenty of space around the edges of your design. With a repeat pattern like the one shown here, make sure that your shapes are not too close together.

1.

2.

Very carefully use a craft knife to cut out your shapes. You should not need to press very hard. Be sure to use a cutting mat under the freezer paper. Otherwise, the knife will cut into your table! That would be really, really bad, so be careful.

WATCH OUT!
Craft knives are super sharp! Please be careful using one, and ask an adult for help.

3.

Iron your tote bag nice and smooth. Center the freezer paper on the bag, with the shiny side facing down. Very carefully iron the paper onto the fabric so it sticks. Make sure that every little corner is firmly stuck. If the paper is not stuck down properly, the paint may bleed under the stencil and mess up your fab design!

4.

Apply a thin layer of paint with the stencil brush. Use only a small amount of paint so it doesn't run. Dab the brush with an up-and-down motion.

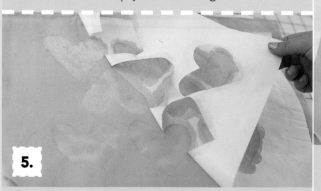

5.

Wait a couple of hours until the paint is dry to the touch. Then peel off the paper. Ta-da!

Hang the piece outside or in a warm spot in your house for a day or two to let it dry completely. Iron over your design to set the paint. Now you will be able to wash your piece if you accidently have a spill!

Use

I Heart Music MP3 Player Case

Finished size: 3½″ × 6″

what do I need?

- 1 piece of red felt at least 6″ × 10″
- 1 piece of white felt at least 3″ × 3″
- Double-sided fusible web at least 3″ × 3″
- Button
- Sewing machine
- Basic supplies (Refer to pages 12 and 14.)

special skills

- Using patterns (page 18)
- Using fusible web (page 19)
- Sewing on a button (page 21)
- Using an iron (page 22)
- Sewing around a corner (page 23)

Prepare the pieces

Heart and tab patterns are on page 167.

1. Cut 2 pieces of red felt 4″ × 6″ for the case back and front.

2. Trace the tab pattern onto parchment paper. Pin the pattern to the red felt, and cut out the tab.

3. Trace the heart pattern on the paper side of the fusible web.

4. With the paper side up, iron the fusible web heart to the white felt. Cut out the heart.

Let's make it!

1.

Peel the paper off the fusible web. Center the heart, sticky side down, on the front of a 4″ × 6″ felt piece. Carefully iron it on.

I heart music, you heart music—**we all heart music.** Let's all love it even more with this super-cool MP3 player case made from colorful felt!

2.

Sew around the heart. Sew slowly, close to the edge of the heart. When you get to the point of the heart, just treat it as if you were sewing around a corner. Put the needle down into the felt, lift the presser foot, and turn the felt. Put the presser foot back down, and keep on going. You can use thread in cream, white, or a pretty color.

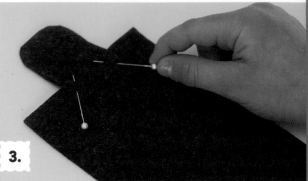

3.

Now, let's attach the tab. Fold the 4″ × 6″ felt piece for the case back in half lengthwise to find the center. Pin the tab at this center point. Place the tab so that it is overlapping about ¼″–½″ on the back of the case.

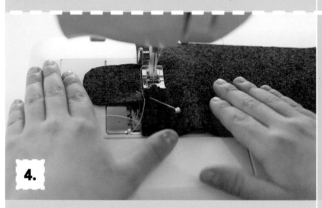

4.

Sew around the area where the tab overlaps the back. Sew close to the edge of the tab in a rectangular shape.

5.

Lay the case front and back right sides together. Pin on 3 sides, leaving the top open.

6.

Sew around the 3 sides with the edge of the presser foot on the edge of the felt. Backstitch at the beginning and end.

7.

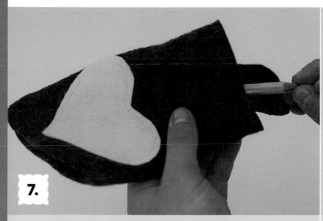

Turn the case right side out. Use the eraser end of a pencil to push out the corners.

8.

Mark the spot on the case front for the button. Using button thread, hand sew it in place.

9.

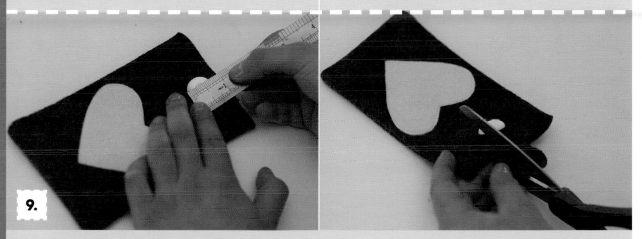

To make the buttonhole in the tab, first measure across the button. With sharp scissors, carefully cut the slit in the tab a little shorter than the button's width. (Felt can stretch a little!) Remember to be careful and not to cut the hole too big. You could always mark it with your disappearing-ink marker.

Pop your MP3 player in the case, and do a little dance. Hooray!

I Heart Music MP3 Player Case

Zippy Pouch

Finished size: 8½″ × 6½″   **Fabrics:** Birch Fabrics, Premier Prints

what do I need?

- ¼ yard of fun printed fabric for the outside

- ¼ yard of fabric for the lining (I used another fun print!)

- 9″ zipper

- Embroidery thread for the zipper pull (*optional*)

- Yarn for the zipper pull (*optional*)

- Sewing machine and zipper foot

- Basic supplies (Refer to pages 12 and 14.)

⤑ special skills

- Using an iron (page 22)

- Sewing around a corner (page 23)

Prepare the pieces

1. Cut 2 pieces of printed fabric 7″ × 9″ for the outside bag.

2. Cut 2 pieces of lining fabric 7″ × 9″.

Let's make it!

1.

Lay 1 lining piece and 1 outside bag piece *wrong* sides together. (We usually do everything with right sides together. Not this time!) Pin them together. This picture shows the outside piece on top.

I personally can never have enough bags! This little cutie is perfect for carrying everything a girl could possibly need. You could fit your whole lip gloss collection in here! In this project, you'll learn to sew in a zipper.

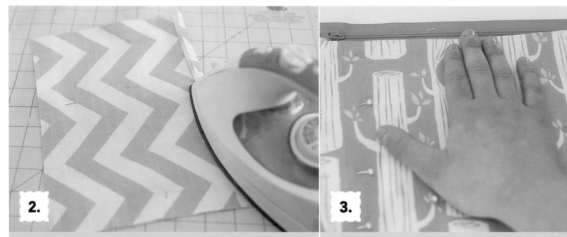

2.

Fold down both layers together ¼″ at the top edge. Fold them onto the lining side. (The photo shows the lining side.) Iron them flat. Do the same thing with the other 2 pieces.

3.

Lay the zipper right side up. (The right side of the zipper is the side with the zipper pull on it.) Lay the folded edge of 1 pouch piece, lining side down, over the fabric part of the zipper next to one side of the zipper teeth.

4. & 5.

Carefully pin the fabric piece to the zipper.

Repeat Steps 3 and 4 with the other pouch piece. Pin this piece to the opposite side of the zipper teeth.

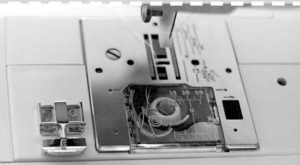

6.

Now attach the zipper foot to your sewing machine. This is a good time to pull out your sewing machine manual to see how. Ask an adult for help if you need to! Attach the foot so that the needle is on the right-hand side so it will be close to the zipper teeth when you sew.

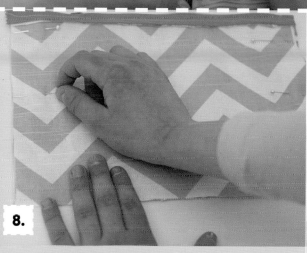

Carefully sew all the way down both sides of the zipper. Make sure to have the edge of the zipper foot butted up to the edge of the zipper teeth. When you are finished, change back to the regular presser foot.

7.

8.

Unzip the zipper. You may think that it would be easier to keep the pouch zipped at this point, but you really need to leave it open so you can turn it right side out later. Fold the pouch out so that the right sides are facing. Pin around the sides and bottom.

9.

Now sew all 3 sides with the edge of the presser foot on the edge of the fabric. Make sure to start and end with a backstitch.

10.

Trim the points off the corners. Don't cut into your stitching! Trim all those pesky threads.

11.

Turn the pouch right side out. You may want to iron it, to make it look super sharp!

ADD A POM-POM

Do you want to add a cute pom-pom? Check out the craft section at your local hobby store. You will be amazed at all the fun colors and sizes available! Insert a length of embroidery floss through the little hole in the zipper pull. Pull the tails even, and attach a pom-pom with a couple of hand stitches.

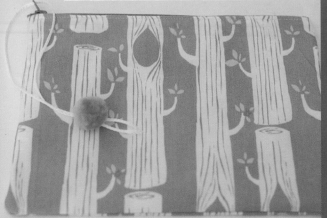

Super-Secret Journal Cover

Finished size: 15″ × 10″

Fabrics: Washi by Rashida Coleman-Hale for Timeless Treasures • Amy Butler

what do I need?

- ½ yard of printed cotton fabric for the outside cover
- ½ yard of fabric for the inside cover
- 1 yard of ½″-wide ribbon
- 4 felt scraps each at least 2″ × 2″ for the flowers
- Small pom-poms (Find them at a craft supply store.)

- Marble composition book, 7½″ × 9¾″ *
- Sewing machine
- Basic supplies (Refer to pages 12 and 14.)

* These are the black notebooks with ruled pages that you can find in any office supply store.

special skills

- Using patterns (page 18)
- Using an iron (page 22)
- Using a hot glue gun (page 22)
- Sewing around a corner (page 23)

Prepare the pieces

Flower pattern is on page 167.

1. Cut 2 pieces of print fabric 11½″ × 26¼″. These will be the front and inside cover.

2. Trace the flower pattern, and cut 4 flowers out of felt.

We all need somewhere to keep our secrets. Now you can keep yours in a notebook with your very own handmade cover. Keep it secure with a ribbon that you wrap and tie around it.

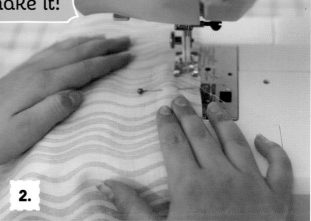

Let's make it!

1.

Place the front and inside pieces right sides together. Pin all the way around. Measure 3″ along the bottom edge. Use the disappearing-ink marker to mark a 3″ line. You will leave this 3″ unsewn so you can turn the cover right side out through the hole.

2.

With the edge of the presser foot on the edge of the fabric, sew all the way around the rectangle. Sew as straight as you can! Stitch from the top of the right side around the corner to the beginning of your 3″ mark. Backstitch. Start stitching again at the end of the marked line. Stitch back to where you began. Remember to backstitch each time you start and stop.

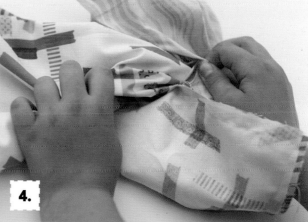

3.

Cut the points off all 4 corners. Don't cut your stitching!

4.

Turn the cover right side out, and iron it. Be sure to fold in the open edge, and iron it neatly.

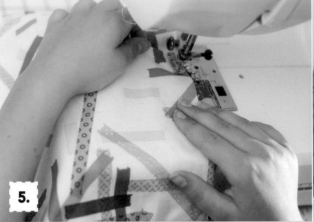

5.

Time to sew it closed. Make sure to sew nice and close to the edge.

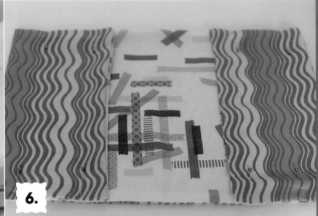

6.

With outside fabrics facing, fold in one side of the piece of fabric 5″, and iron it in place. Repeat this with the other side. This will create the inside flaps. Now pin both flaps in place.

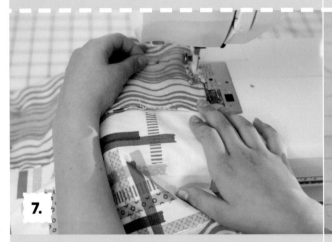

7.

Sew close to the edges on each folded end. You will need to sew about ⅛″ from the edge of the fabric. Sew nice and straight! Repeat this with the other end.

8. & 9.

Turn the book cover ends right side out. Use a chopstick to push out the corners.

Give your cover a good iron to make it nice and flat.

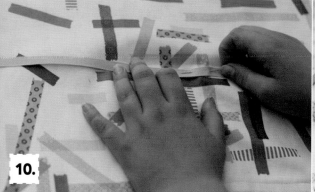

10.

Fold the piece of ribbon in half to find the middle. Do the same with the cover. Pin the ribbon to the center of the outside of the cover.

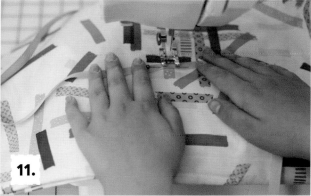

11.

Sew on the ribbon at this center point. Sew it in place securely.

12.

Put a dab of hot glue on 2 felt flowers. Sandwich them together with a ribbon end in between. Repeat with the 2 other flowers and the other ribbon end.

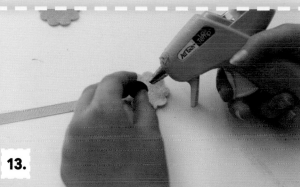

13.

Carefully hot glue the small pom-poms to each side of the flowers.

Now put the cover on your book, and start writing your secrets! Just remember to hide it away somewhere safe!

Happiness Storage Trays

Finished size: *6˝ × 6˝*   **Fabrics:** Joel Dewberry • Far Far Away by Heather Ross

what do I need?

- Piece of quilting-weight cotton print fabric at least 10˝ × 10˝ for the inside of the tray

- Piece of heavyweight cotton print fabric at least 10˝ × 10˝ for the outside of the tray*

- Piece of cotton batting at least 10˝ × 10˝

- 8 assorted fun flat buttons (with holes)

- Sewing machine

- Basic supplies (Refer to pages 12 and 14.)

* The heavier fabric on the outside helps make the tray nice and stiff.

special skills

- Sewing on a button (page 21)

- Using an iron (page 22)

- Sewing around a corner (page 23)

- Topstitch (page 23)

Prepare the pieces

1. Cut a 9˝ × 9˝ square from each of the 2 fabrics. Cut 1 from the batting, too.

2. Make a sandwich with the squares. Lay the batting on the bottom. Put the outside fabric square over it, right side facing up. Then put the inside fabric on top, with the right side down.

Batting ---▸

Outside fabric ----

Inside fabric ----

These cute-as-a-button little trays are perfect for storing all your little treasures. **Make a few to hold your favorite collections!**

Let's make it!

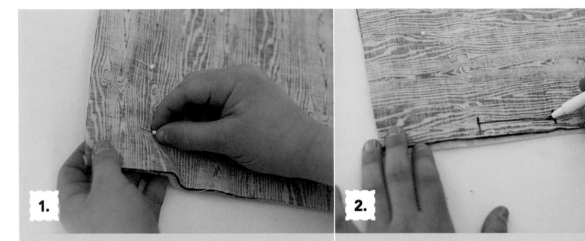

1.
Make sure the pieces are lined up square. Pin around all 4 sides.

2.
Use the disappearing-ink marker to draw a 3″ line centered along one edge.

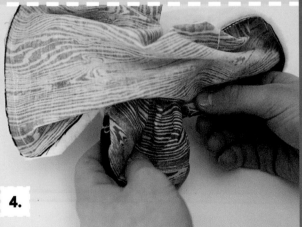

3.
Sew the pieces together. Sew with the edge of the presser foot on the edge of the fabric. Start at the top corner. Sew down to the bottom corner, and turn. Sew across the bottom to the beginning of the marked line. Start stitching again at the other end of the line; sew up the other side and around to the starting corner. Don't forget to backstitch at each start and stop!

4.
Sometimes the corners can seem a little bulky, so you may want to trim the corners. Do not cut into the stitching! Turn your tray right side out. The batting should be on the inside of the tray!

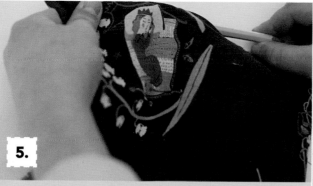

5. Use the eraser end of a pencil to push out the corners so they are nice and neat.

6. Time to turn on the iron. Carefully fold in the edges that are still open. Pin them in place. Iron the entire tray so it looks super neat and flat.

7. Topstitch ¼˝ from the edge all the way around the square. This will make the edge look neat. It also closes up the opening in the edge of the square.

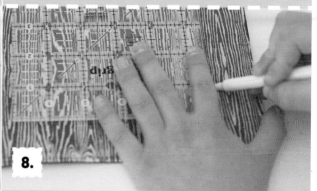

8. Mark a 6˝ × 6˝ square exactly in the center of the square you have just sewn. Use your disappearing-ink marker. Hint: You can use a 6˝ square ruler as shown here. Or just measure with a regular ruler. Ask an adult for help.

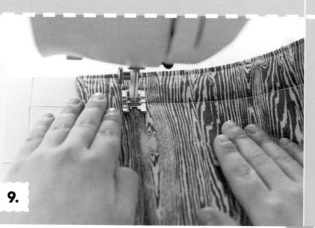

9. Before the disappearing ink actually disappears, sew around the square that you just marked.

10.

Using your disappearing-ink marker and a ruler, draw a line from a corner of the inner stitching to the corner of the square. This will be your guide for folding the corner. Repeat in the other 3 corners.

11.

Make a fold at a corner. (Look closely at the photo.) Make sure the top edges of the tray look even. Pin to hold the fold in place. Do this with all the corners.

12.

Imagine a line going from the bottom corner of the tray straight up. Find the halfway point, and mark it with a dot. This will be the button spot.

13. & 14.

Use button thread in your needle. Push the needle and thread through one side of the folded corner, and then push it back through to the first side. Leave a nice long tail. Tie the tail and needle thread together with a knot. Be sure to pull tight to hold the corner together.

Now push your needle through the hole of 1 button, and sew back through the second hole to the other side of the corner.

15.

Now add another button to the other side of the corner. Go up through the first hole and then down through the remaining hole on that button and carefully back through to the side you started from.

16.

Tie a knot using the thread and the tail you left from the knot. Make sure to tie the knot behind the button and trim the thread so it doesn't show. It sounds complicated, but it really isn't! Be careful not to prick your fingers! Now do this with the remaining corners.

Yippee-ki-yay ... you did it! Don't you just love your super-cute tray?

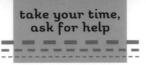

Save Your Pennies Purse

Finished size: 4″ × 4½″

Fabrics: Washi by Rashida Coleman-Hale for Timeless Treasures • Far Far Away by Heather Ross

what do I need?

- ¼ yard of fabric for the outside and the pocket (Look for a light decorator-weight fabric.)

- ¼ yard of fabric for the lining

- Fun button or thrift store earring

- 1 snap (I like to use snap fastener kits by Dritz. They come with a handy tool to make the snaps easy to apply.)

- Hot glue gun and gluestick

- Sewing machine

- Basic supplies (Refer to pages 12 and 14.)

special skills

- Using patterns (page 18)

- Using an iron (page 22)

- Using a hot glue gun (page 22)

- Topstitch (page 23)

- Sewing around a corner (page 23)

Prepare the pieces

Purse tab pattern is on page 167.

1. Cut 3 pieces of fabric 5″ × 10″ for the outside and the pocket.

2. Cut 2 pieces of fabric 5″ × 10″ for the lining.

3. Trace the pattern, and cut 2 tabs from the outside fabric.

Here is the perfect place to store all that hard-earned allowance. There's room in the handy inside pocket for your gift card stash, too!

Let's make it!

This purse has a pretty lining and closes with a tab
to keep your pennies safe and sound.

TAB

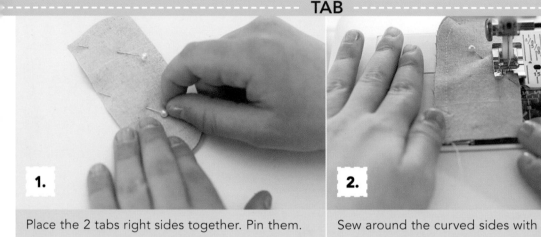

1. Place the 2 tabs right sides together. Pin them.

2. Sew around the curved sides with the edge of the presser foot on the edge of the fabric. Leave the straight edge open for turning.

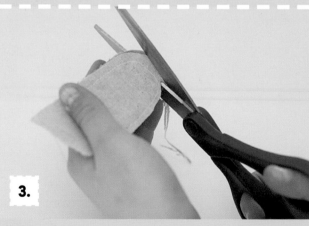

3. Trim around the curve. Don't cut your stitching!

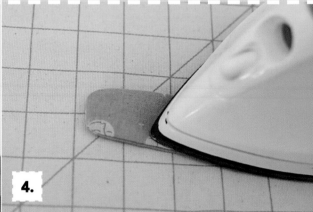

4. Turn the tab right side out, and iron it. Set it aside.

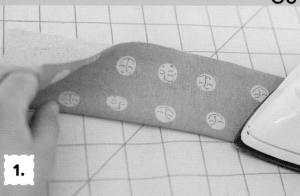

1.

To make the pocket, fold 1 of the outside fabric pieces in half along the length, wrong sides together. Iron it.

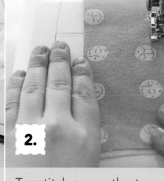

2.

Topstitch across the top folded edge. Sew with the edge of the presser foot on the edge of the fabric.

STRAIGHT STITCHING

Stitch as straight as you can—this stitching will show! It may help to mark the lines first with a disappearing-ink marker.

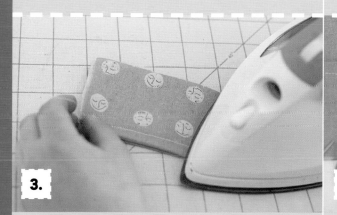

3.

Fold the entire pocket in half crosswise, and iron it. (Make sure it is folded exactly in half.)

4.

Unfold the pocket and pin it to the outside fabric piece, lining up the raw edges.

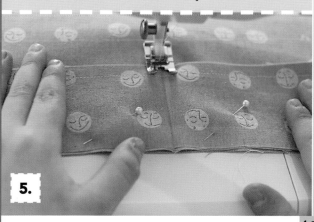

5.

Using the fold as your guide, sew down the center of the pocket. Backstitch at the beginning and end.

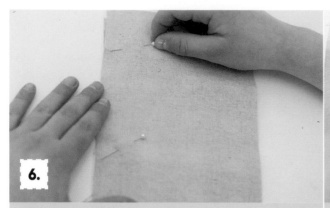

6.

Place a lining piece and outside piece right sides together. Pin across the top. One of the front pieces will be the piece with the pocket. Make sure to sew across the top of that piece and not across the pocket.

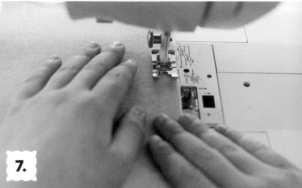

7.

Sew with the edge of the presser foot on the edge of the fabric across the top where you pinned.

8.

Open the piece out, and iron it nice and flat. Do the same with the other lining and outside pieces.

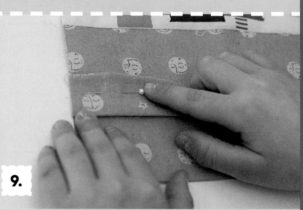

9.

Pin the tab in place at the center of one end of the outside piece. It should be facing inward.

1.

Place the 2 large purse pieces right sides together, matching lining to lining and outside fabric to outside fabric. Starting at the side seams, pin all the way around. (Make sure the sewn seams line up perfectly.)

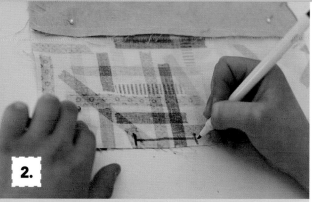

2.

Mark a 2″ space in the bottom of the lining. This will be your no-sew zone!

3.

Sew all the way around (except leave an opening for the no-sew zone). If you don't remember how to do the no-sew zone, see Cross-Body Handy Pouch, Steps 1 and 2 (page 66).

4.

Turn the purse right side out. Iron it so it is lovely and flat.

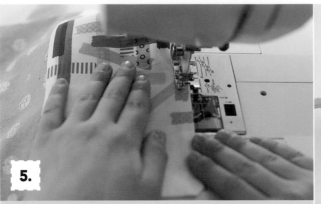

5.

Fold the edges of the opening in, and iron. Topstitch the opening closed nice and close to the edge.

6.

Push the lining inside the outside purse. You may need to iron it again!

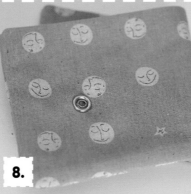

7.

Using the tab pattern as a guide, mark the spots for the 2 pieces of the snap on the purse and the tab.

8.

Follow the directions on the snap package to attach the snap.

9.

Use hot glue to attach your button over the spot on the outside of the tab where you attached the snap. Let it dry for a few minutes.

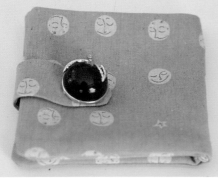

Now offer to do some extra chores around the house. Maybe Mom or Dad will help you fill up your new purse!

Paint It Yourself Pillow

what do I need?

- ½ yard natural-colored cotton canvas fabric for the pillow front*

- ½ yard fun patterned fabric for the pillow back (quilter's cotton or lightweight decorator cotton)

- Fabric paint in assorted colors (I like DecoArt SoSoft Fabric Acrylics.)

- Paintbrush and paint tray

- Fiberfill stuffing (Find it at a fabric store.)

- Sewing machine

- Basic supplies (Refer to pages 12 and 14.)

If you're creating your own design, make sure the fabric is at least 6″ wider and 6″ longer than your design.

special skills

- Using patterns (page 18)

- Whipstitch (page 20)

- Using an iron (page 22)

Prepare the pieces

Bird pattern is on pages 168 and 169.

1. Prewash and dry your natural cotton canvas fabric. You will probably need to iron it once it's dry.

2. Trace the 2 parts of the bird pattern, tape them together along the dotted line, and cut out the pattern as one piece. Center the pattern on the canvas, leaving at least 3″ of space all around the design. Use a disappearing-ink marker or pencil to trace around it onto the canvas. If you want to create your own design, draw it on paper. Then transfer it onto the fabric.

3. Once you have traced around the body of the bird, you can cut out the wing and face pieces to trace around.

This hand-painted
pillow is sure to be a
showstopper! You can
make a bird like this one,
or make your own design.
Try a fish or an apple.
I'm sure you won't be
able to stop at just one.
Tweet, tweet!

Let's make it!

The pillow will be the same shape as your design. The unpainted part of the fabric will make a border around it.

1.

Use fabric paints to color your design. Use the paint sparingly so it doesn't take forever to dry. Even so, let it dry for at least 24 hours.

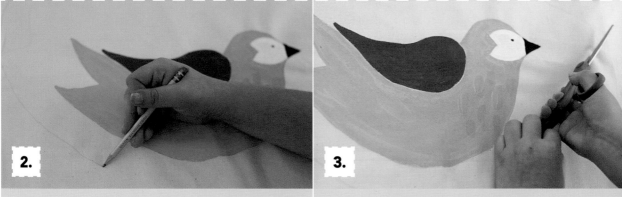

2.

With a pencil, draw all around your design, about 3″ away from the edges. This will allow space for sewing.

3.

Now cut out the canvas on your drawn lines.

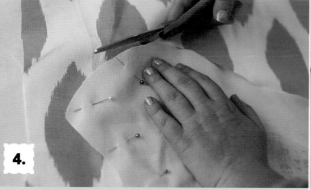

4.

Lay the pillow back fabric faceup. Place your cutout design facedown on the backing fabric, and pin it in place. Carefully cut it out around the edges of the cutout design.

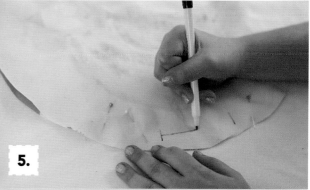

5.

Use your disappearing-ink marker to draw a 3″ line along the bottom. This will be the hole for stuffing.

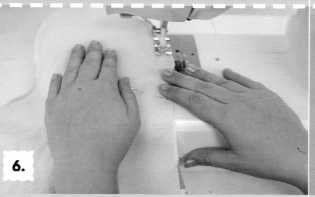

6.

With the edge of the presser foot on the edge of the fabric, carefully sew around the pillow. Stop at the beginning of your marked 3″ line. Start stitching again at the other end. Make sure to backstitch at every start and stop!

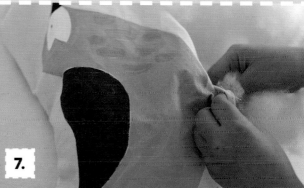

7.

Turn your pillow right side out. Using small tufts of fiberfill, start stuffing the pillow. Stuff until the pillow feels nice and plump. Make sure the fiberfill goes into all the corners.

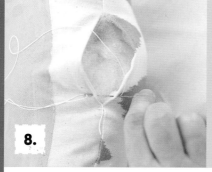

8.

Time to use those hand sewing skills. Use a whipstitch to sew the opening closed. Remember to finish off with a knot.

You did it!

113

Hoop Treats

Finished size: 6″

what do I need?

Makes 1 hoop treat.

- 1 piece of cotton canvas fabric measuring at least 8″ × 8″

- Small scraps of 3 different fabrics for the design

- Double-sided fusible web

- Little piece of ribbon

- 6″ wooden embroidery hoop (Find it at a fabric or craft store.)

- Sewing machine

- Basic supplies (Refer to pages 12 and 14.)

special skills

- Using patterns (page 18)

- Using fusible web (page 19)

- Using an iron (page 22)

Prepare the pieces

Cupcake and mushroom patterns are on pages 168 and 169.

1. Trace your chosen pattern pieces onto the paper side of the fusible web. (The mushroom and cupcake each have 3 pieces.)

2. Follow the directions on the package to iron the fusible web (with the rough side of the web down) onto your fabrics.

3. Cut out the pieces.

Let's make it!

1.

Carefully peel off the backing paper from your fabric shapes.

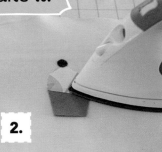

2.

Position them on the canvas fabric, sticky side down. Try to center the design, but if you're off a little, that's okay. Iron the pieces in place.

What could be cuter than a little framed mushroom or cupcake? These projects are a great way to use little scraps of your favorite fabrics. **Better watch out—you won't be able to stop at just one!**

3.

Thread your machine needle and bobbin with black thread. Sew close to the edge around your design. It doesn't have to look perfect. If you want to, stitch some up-and-down lines on the cupcake "paper." Look at the pictures for a guide.

4.

Take apart the wooden hoop, and lay the inner piece on a table. Center the canvas on top. Loosen the outer hoop screw (not too loose). Gently push it onto the canvas and inner hoop with the hoop's screw at the top.

5.

Pull gently on the fabric to keep it taut and wrinkle free. Tighten the screw to hold everything in place.

6. & 7.

Check that it all looks good. Then carefully trim off the excess fabric around the back of the hoop.

Tie on a ribbon, and hang it on your wall!

What other things could you find to use as a frame? Start thinking creatively!

Silhouette Pillow

Finished size: 20″ × 20″   **Fabrics:** Amy Butler • Premier Prints

what do I need?

- 1 yard of printed quilting or decorator-weight cotton for pillow
- 8″ × 11″ piece of colored felt for silhouette (Black looks great!)
- 20″ × 20″ pillow form (Find it at a fabric store.)
- 8″ × 11″ piece of double-sided fusible web
- Black Sharpie marker
- Digital camera
- Computer and printer
- Sewing machine
- Basic supplies (Refer to pages 12 and 14.)

special skills

- Using fusible web (page 19)
- Whipstitch (page 20)
- Using an iron (page 22)
- Sewing around a corner (page 23)

Prepare the pieces

1. Have someone take your picture. The photo should show your profile from the chest up. Be sure the image takes up most of the frame. It works best if you stand against a white background.

2. Ask an adult to help you load the photo onto your computer. Use the computer to enlarge the photo to fit 8½″ × 11″ paper. Print it out in black and white, on regular printer paper. You'll know your image is big enough if it takes up most of the page. The perfect height of the picture should be around 9½″–10″.

3. With a black Sharpie, carefully outline your profile image. Take extra care around the face area. You want it to look like you!

4. Using sharp paper scissors, cut out your silhouette. It can be a little hard to cut those edges around the face, so ask for help if you need to. Now you have a pattern!

5. For the front of the pillow, cut a square of the printed cotton 20″ × 20″.

6. For the back of the pillow, cut 2 pieces of fabric 15″ × 20″.

Fancy your face on a pillow? Why not make a whole family? These totally cute and personality-filled pillows will have you seeing double.

Let's make it!

You'll make your felt silhouette and then create the pillow.

---------- **SILHOUETTE** ----------

1.
Place the fusible web paper side up on a flat surface. Lay your pattern on top. Place the pattern facedown so your silhouette will be looking in the same direction as in the photo. Carefully trace around your image.

2.
Now lay the marked fusible web on the black felt, with the rough side of the web down. Follow the directions on the package to iron it on.

3.
With a sharp pair of scissors, very carefully cut out your silhouette. Yay! That is your silhouette done!

---------- **PILLOW** ----------

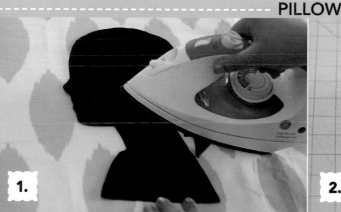

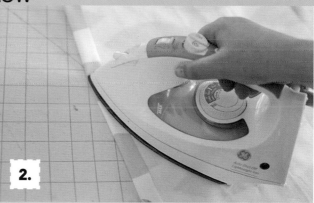

1.
Peel the backing paper off the fusible web on your silhouette. Iron the silhouette onto the center of the pillow front. Set it aside.

2.
On 1 of the pillow back pieces, fold over the edge of the long side about ½˝. Iron along the fold. Fold it over again, iron the fold, and pin it in place. Repeat with the second back piece.

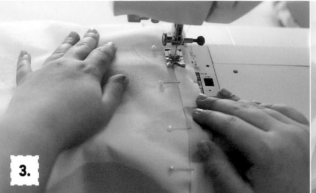

3.

Sew down the fold on both pieces. Try to sew close to the edge.

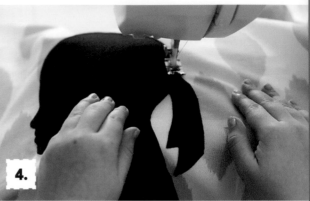

4.

Change your needle and bobbin thread to black. (If your stitches get a little higgledy-piggledy, it will be harder to see!) Sew close to the edge all the way around your silhouette.

5.

Now let's put it all together. Lay the pillow front piece faceup. Then lay 1 back piece right side down on top of the front piece. Line up the top, bottom, and one side edge. Lay the other back piece right side down on top of the stack. Line up the remaining raw edges. The hemmed edges of the back pieces are supposed to overlap, so don't worry!

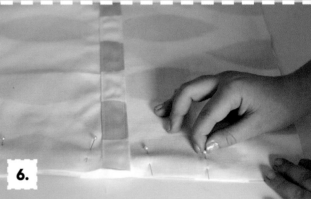

6.

Pin around all 4 edges of the pillow.

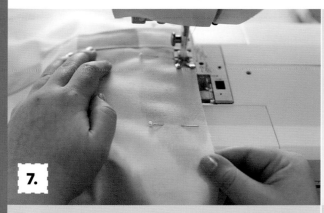

7.

With the edge of the presser foot on the edge of the fabric, carefully and slowly sew all the way around. Don't forget to backstitch at the beginning and end.

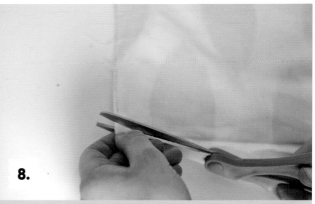

8.

Clip off the points on the corners. Don't cut your stitching! Trim any loose threads.

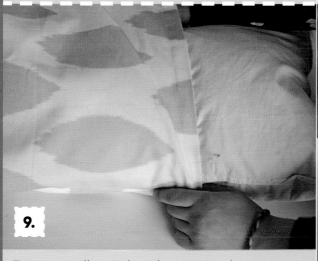

9.

Turn your pillow right side out. Use the eraser end of a pencil to push out the corners. Stuff with the pillow form.

Great job!
Don't you just love your creation?
Wouldn't a dog or cat silhouette
pillow be cute, too?

Fun Name Banner

Finished size: Approximately 110″ long (depending on the number of letters you use)

Fabrics: Anna Maria Horner • Rashida Coleman-Hale • Aneela Hoey • Premier Prints • Heather Bailey

what do I need?

- 2 pieces of cotton fabric 8″ × 10″ for each letter in your name (or word you've chosen)

- A piece of black felt measuring at least 5″ × 5″ for each letter in your banner

- ½ yard or more of double-sided fusible web (You'll need enough to fuse to the black letters.)

- 1 packet of double-fold quilt binding

- Thread to match the binding

- Sewing machine

- Basic supplies (Refer to pages 12 and 14.)

special skills

- Using fusible web (page 19)
- Using an iron (page 22)

Prepare the pieces

1. You will need to cut 2 rectangles measuring 8″ × 10″ for the background of each letter.

2. Using your computer, print out each letter of your name. In Microsoft Word, I used the Arial Black font, size 400. (Ask an adult for help if necessary to set this up.)

3. Cut out the letters.

4. Trace the letter outlines onto the paper side of the fusible web. Important: Place them facedown so you will trace them backward!

Personalize your space with a groovy banner that just screams your name. Maybe you would like a banner that just says "groovy"? **It's up to you, my friend!**

5. Follow the printed directions on the fusible web to iron the letters onto the black felt. (Turn off the steam on your iron.)

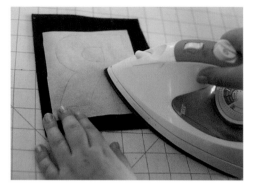

6. Cut out the letters.

FUN ADD-ONS

If you have a short name, such as Ann or Pip, you could maybe add a heart or a star to the beginning and end of your banner. That would look so cute!

Let's make it!

1.

Center the first letter on the lower part of a fabric rectangle. (Leave room at the top for the binding.) Peel the paper backing off the letter, and iron it on well with a hot iron. Repeat with each letter.

2.

Sew around the outside of each of the letters with coordinating thread. Sew very slowly, close to the edge.

3.

Place the rectangle front and back pieces right sides together. Pin around the side and bottom edges. Leave the top open. Check to make sure that the letter is facing the right way up!

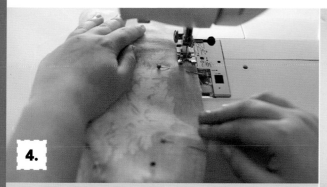

4.

With the edge of the presser foot on the edge of the fabric, sew around the pinned edges. Don't forget to backstitch at the beginning and end.

5.

Turn the rectangle right side out. Push out the corners with the eraser end of a pencil. Iron the rectangle. Do the same thing for all your letters!

6.

Use a ruler and pencil to mark a straight line across the tops of all your banner pieces. Trim them so they are nice and even.

7.

Lay everything on the floor. Open up the folded binding tape. Evenly space the letters inside the fold. Make sure that the tops of the rectangles are butted up inside the fold of the tape. Pin them all in place.

Using machine thread the same color as the binding, slowly sew close to the edge of the open side of the binding. You want to trap the tops of the banners inside. Sew from the beginning of the binding right to the end.

Neaten up the ends, and trim your threads.

You are ready to hang your amazing masterpiece. Imagine one in holiday fabric or even a Halloween theme. What fun!

8.

Scrappy Artwork

Finished size: 9″ × 9″

what do I need?

• At least ½ yard of natural canvas fabric for the background (Make sure that your fabric piece is not only big enough for the bird design but also has space around it to fit into the frame. You should choose your frame before cutting out the canvas fabric.)

• 3 fabric scraps for the bird (The largest scrap should be at least 8″ × 10″. The others can be smaller.)

• Scraps of trim such as ribbon for the bird's wing

• Button for the bird's eye

• ½ yard of double-sided fusible web (or a piece large enough to back the bird pieces)

• Scrap of felt for the bird's head

• Large picture frame (I used a 20″ × 20″ frame, but you can choose a frame in the size and shape you love.)

• Sewing machine

• Basic supplies (Refer to pages 12 and 14.)

special skills

• Using patterns (page 18)

• Using fusible web (page 19)

• Sewing on a button (page 21)

• Using an iron (page 22)

Prepare the pieces

Bird pattern pieces are on pages 170 and 171.

1. Trace the parts of the bird body pattern pieces and tape them together along the dotted lines. Trace the one pattern onto the paper side of the fusible web. Also trace the wing onto fusible web. Roughly cut around the traced pieces.

2. Decide which fabrics you want to use for the head, beak, body, and wing. (I used plain fabric for the wing and covered it with rows of ribbon trim.)

FRAME FINDS
Thrift shops are a great place to find old picture frames. Usually all they need is a new coat of paint!

Become the Picasso of poplin or the Van Gogh of velvet with these super-cool and creative scrappy artworks. I've given you a pattern and directions for the bird. But feel free to do it your way. I made the one shown in the photo 9" square, but you can make it whatever size and shape you want! **Thinking creatively is a "requirement" for this fun project!**

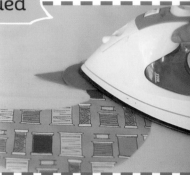

3. Iron the fusible web, with the rough side down, onto the fabric and felt you've chosen. (Be sure to turn off the steam on the iron.) Cut out the pieces.

4. Iron your piece of cotton canvas fabric. Lay the bird body, head, and back pieces in the center. (You will add the wing later.) Once they are exactly where you want them, iron them in place.

Let's make it!

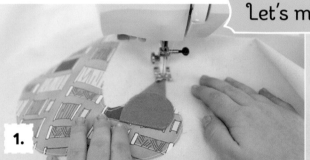

1.

Using your choice of thread color, stitch around each part of the bird's body. Try to make sure that your stitching is even and close to the edge of the fabric.

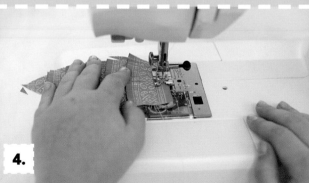

2.

Now to sew the wing. Decide how you would like to decorate it. You could leave it plain or create a cool effect by adding layers of cut-up ribbon, felt, or even fabric scraps. I love that this kind of addition gives a little texture to the artwork, and it really will show your creativity too!

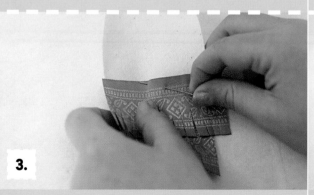

3.

Pin the trim of your choice to the wing piece.

4.

Sew the trim in place a row at a time. Sew across only the top of each row so the lower part is loose like feathers.

5.

Trim all the straggly bits off to make the wing shaped the same as the pattern.

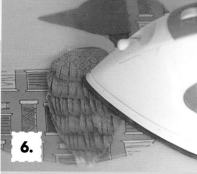

6.

Iron the wing in place.

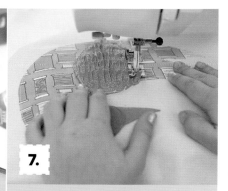

7.

Sew around the wing nice and slowly.

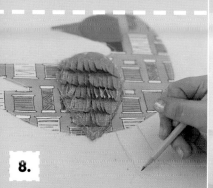

8.

Draw some legs with a pencil.

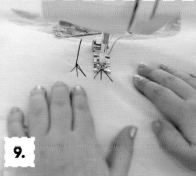

9.

Using black thread, sew on the lines. Get creative here!

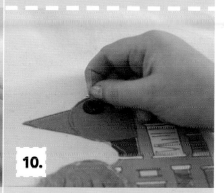

10.

All that should be left is to sew on the button eye. Pick a cute, interesting one!

Frame it!

1. To prepare the fabric for the frame, iron it nice and flat.

2. A new frame usually has a mat and a piece of cardboard backing. Cut your canvas a couple of inches wider all around than the mat. Tape it to the back of the mat with blue painter's tape or masking tape.

If you are using a frame without a mat, wrap the fabric around a piece of cardboard that is cut to fit the frame. Secure it with masking tape.

Don't just stop at a bird. Make a whole zoo of fabric art!

Raise the Flag Quilt

Finished size: About 31″ × 39″

Fabrics: Anna Maria Horner • Denyse Schmidt • Joel Dewberry • Jay McCarroll • Alexander Henry

what do I need?

- ½ yard each of 3 different cotton fabrics
- ½ yard of fabric for the canton (the upper left corner of the flag)
- 1¼ yards of fabric for the flag back
- ¼ yard of felt for the stars
- Package of craft-size cotton quilt batting (or a piece 34″ × 45″)*
- ¾ yard double-sided fusible web
- 2 ribbon scraps for hanging your quilt
- Sewing machine
- Basic supplies (Refer to pages 12 and 14.)

I like cotton because it is thinner and gives the flag just the right amount of weight and not too much fluffiness.

special skills

- Using patterns (page 18)
- Using fusible web (page 19)
- Using an iron (page 22)

Prepare the pieces

Star pattern is on page 167.

1. Cut 13 strips each measuring 3″ × 39″. Cut 4 strips each from 2 of the fabrics and 5 strips out of the third fabric.

2. Cut 1 rectangle 15½″ × 20½″ out of plain colored fabric for the canton (upper left corner) of the flag.

3. Cut a piece of fabric for the flag back measuring 36″ × 44″.

4. & 5. Trace 50 stars onto the paper side of the fusible web. Place the rough side of the web down on the back of the felt, and iron.

6. Start cutting 50 stars!

Show how patriotic and crafty you are with this crazy, patchy flag. Once you get the hang of it, try your hand at making flags from other countries!

Let's make it!

1. Lay out all your fabric strips in the order you like. Place 2 strips right sides together. Pin in place.

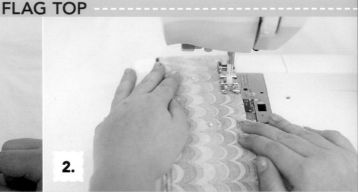

2. Sew together along one long side with the edge of the presser foot on the edge of the fabric.

3. Iron the strips open.

4. Attach the next strip, and continue as before.

5. Continue adding all the strips and ironing until all 13 are sewn together.

6. Lay the canton piece right side down on your ironing board. Fold in ½˝ on all 4 edges, and iron in place.

7.

Peel the paper off the back of the stars.

8.

Position the stars on the canton, leaving a little room around the edges of the fabric rectangle. It will be tough to make them all fit, but I know you can do it!

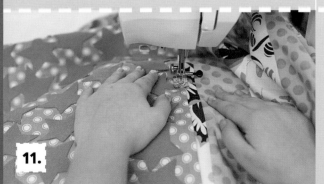

9.

Iron them in place with a hot iron.

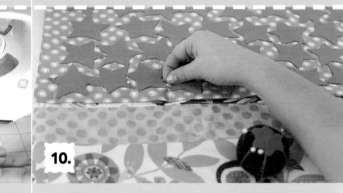

10.

Lay the rectangle in the upper left-hand corner of your flag, and pin it in place.

11.

Sew close to the edge around the entire rectangle.

1.

Lay your flag top on top of the cotton batting. Cut the batting to the same size as the flag top.

2.

Lay out the flag back wrong side up. Lay the flag top and batting on top of the flag back. Use your ruler and disappearing-ink marker to draw a line on the backing fabric 2″ away from the edge of the quilt top. Do this on all 4 edges. Cut the quilt back along the drawn line.

3.

Fold a 1″ edge of the flag back to the front. Repeat with the opposite edge.

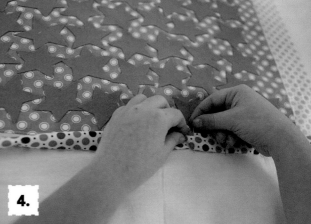

4.

Fold the edges another 1″ to cover the edges of the flag. Pin the folds in place. Repeat Steps 3 and 4 with the 2 remaining back edges.

5. Once it's all pinned, iron it!

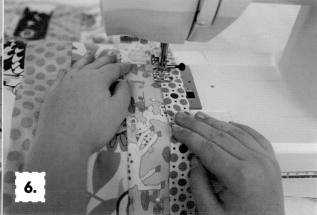

6. Sew nice and close to the inner folded edge of the banner. Keep your stitching straight as can be!

7. Make 2 loops from the little ribbon scraps. Pin them to the top back edge of your flag for hanging.

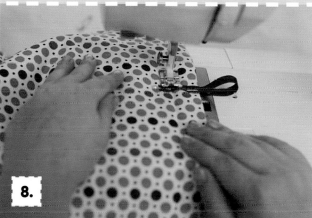

8. Sew the loops in place using your sewing machine.

Hang your beautifully patchy flag in a place of honor. Above your bed will look super!

Strawberry Patch Bookends

Finished size: About 9″ tall • **Fabrics:** Michael Miller

what do I need?

Makes 1 bookend.

- ½ yard of printed quilting cotton
- 10″ × 10″ piece of felt for the leaf
- Scrap of felt for the stem
- Embroidery floss to match the felt
- Fiberfill stuffing (Find it at a fabric store.)
- 2 pounds of rice for stuffing
- Sewing machine
- Hot glue gun and gluestick
- Basic supplies (Refer to pages 12 and 14.)

special skills

- Using patterns (page 18)
- Whipstitch (page 20)
- Using a hot glue gun (page 22)

Prepare the pieces

Strawberry pattern pieces are on pages 172 and 173.

1. Trace both parts of the segment pattern onto parchment paper, and cut it out as one piece. Trace the leaf onto parchment paper.

2. Fold your print fabric in half so the selvage is running down the side. Pin on the strawberry pattern piece. Position it so that it is horizontal across the top of the fabric. Carefully cut it out. Repeat to cut 6 pieces total.

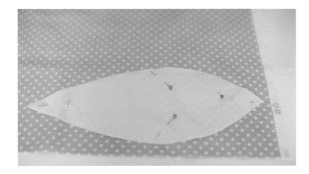

3. Fold the felt in half, pin the dotted edge of the leaf pattern on the fold, and cut it out.

4. Cut a rectangle 1½″ × 4″ of felt for the stem.

These fun and seriously cute bookends will brighten up even the dreariest bookshelf. **Who knew fruit could be so cute?**

Let's make it!

SEW THE PIECES

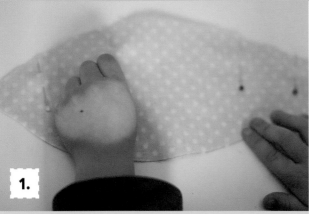

1. Place 2 strawberry pieces right sides together. Pin along one side. The top end of the piece is fatter than the bottom, so make sure the pieces are lined up correctly, with the tops and bottoms matching.

2. With the edge of the presser foot on the edge of the fabric, sew down the length of the strawberry piece. Be careful along the curve. Backstitch at the beginning and again at the end. Repeat Steps 1 and 2 with 2 other pieces.

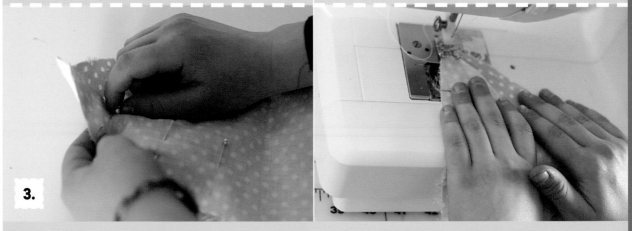

3. Now we're going to attach a third segment to each pair from Step 2. Line up the third segment on one side of one of a pair, making sure the tops are facing in the same direction. Pin carefully, and sew. Again, repeat this with the other pair. This is a little tricky, so sew like a snail! You now have 2 half-strawberries.

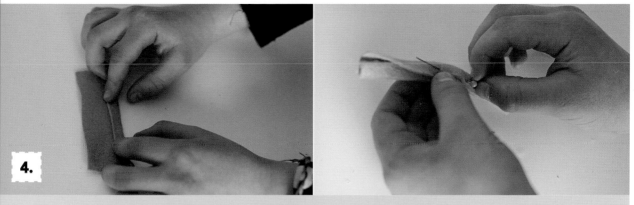

4.

To sew the stem, carefully roll up the piece of felt. Secure it with a pin so it stays tight.

5.

Thread an embroidery needle with matching embroidery thread. Sew a whipstitch to secure the stem. Remember to start with a knot.

6.

Center the stem at the top of a half-strawberry. Remember, the top is the fatter end. Pin the stem to the right (patterned) side of the fabric. Make sure it is pointing down. If you get stuck, look at the photo as a guide. Secure the stem with a pin.

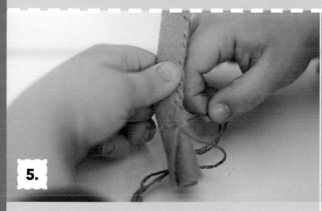

7.

Place the strawberry halves right sides together, and carefully pin the edges around the whole strawberry. Mark a 2″ gap for stuffing close to the top with your disappearing-ink marker.

8.

Sew around the strawberry.

Strawberry Patch Bookends

1. Very carefully turn the strawberry right side out. Time to raid the pantry! Ask an adult to help you hold the hole open, and fill the strawberry one-third to one-half full with rice. Use a rolled-up piece of paper or a funnel for this part.

2. Using small tufts of fiberfill, start stuffing the rest of the strawberry. Make sure to fill every little nook and cranny.

3. Thread a sewing needle with button thread. Sew up the hole using a whipstitch.

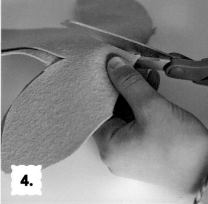

4. Fold the leaf piece in half, and carefully snip a tiny hole right in the center.

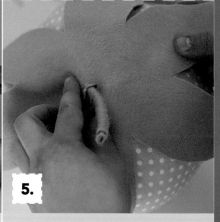

5. Place the leaf on top of the strawberry, and pull the stem through the hole.

Put a dab of hot glue on the tips of the strawberry leaves. Press them in place until the glue is dry.

6.

Ta-da! Take a break. When you are ready, come back and make number 2 of our bookend pair.

Cuddle

Olive Owl

Finished size: 11″ × 13″   **Fabrics:** Joel Dewberry

what do I need?

- ½ yard of bright printed quilting cotton or lightweight decorator fabric for the body

- Scrap of quilting cotton measuring at least 7″ × 7″ for the wings

- Felt scraps in different colors for the inner eyes, outer eyes, beak, feet, feathers, and wings

- 2 large buttons for the eyes

- Fiberfill stuffing (Find it at a fabric store.)

- Sewing machine

- Basic supplies (Refer to pages 12 and 14.)

special skills

- Using patterns (page 18)

- Whipstitch (page 20)

- Sewing on a button (page 21)

- Using an iron (page 22)

Prepare the pieces

Owl patterns are on pages 159–162.

1. Enlarge the body patterns, and then trace the enlargements onto parchment paper and cut them out. Tape the enlarged body bottom pattern to the enlarged body top pattern along the straight edge to make a whole body pattern.

2. Fold your piece of cotton fabric so that the right sides are together.

3. Pin the body pattern on the fabric, and then cut out the pattern pieces. You will have the front and back of the owl.

4. Cut 2 large circles of felt for Olive's outer eyes.

5. Cut 2 smaller circles of felt for Olive's inner eyes.

6. Cut 1 beak from felt.

7. Cut 2 feet pieces from felt.

8. Cut 1 of each feather piece from felt.

9. Cut 2 wing pieces from felt and 2 wing pieces from cotton fabric.

There's nothing like a cute owl stuffie to make your day a little brighter. Olive will be perfectly happy perched on your bed or on a cozy shelf. **Hoot! Hoot!**

BODY

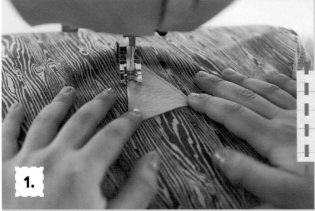

1.

> **EXTRA HELP**
>
> You may want to use fusible web to hold the beak in place before you sew. If you do, see Using Fusible Web (page 19).

Place the beak on the owl's front body. (Look at the pattern or the project photo to see where it goes.) Pin the beak in place, and sew it on, stitching close to the edge.

2.

Place the row of 3-pointed feathers on Olive's front body. Pin it in place.

3.

Sew across the top of the feathers. Sew nice and close to the edge. Repeat to sew the smaller row of feathers overlapping the first row.

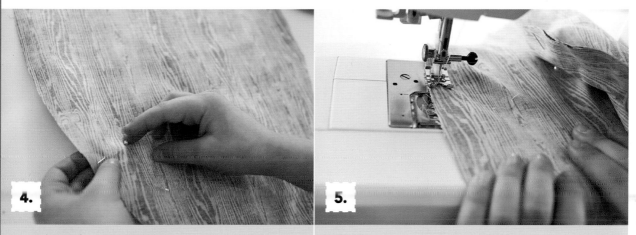

4.

Put Olive's front and back body pieces right sides together. Pin them all the way around. Mark a 3″ line with your disappearing-ink marker at the bottom of Olive. This will be the hole you use to stuff her.

5.

With the edge of the presser foot on the edge of the fabric, sew all the way around. Stop at the beginning of the 3″ line. Start again at the other end. Be sure to backstitch at each start and stop. Sew carefully on the tight curves of Olive's ears. You want them to be pointy.

6.

Turn her right side out.

7.

Using small tufts of fiberfill, start stuffing Olive. Make sure you get enough stuffing in her ears!

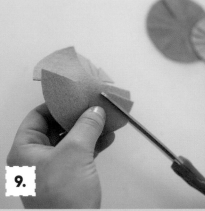

8. Using your best whipstitch, hand stitch the hole closed.

9. Time to add the eyes. I like to cut slits around the outside of both the outer and the inner eye. But you can leave them plain if you like.

10. Sew on a button for each eye, with the felt eye pieces stacked underneath. Look at the pattern for placement.

WINGS AND FEET

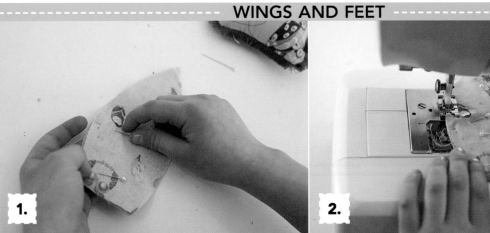

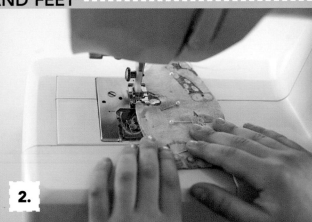

1. Let's tackle the wings! With 1 piece of felt and 1 piece of fabric right sides together, pin all the way around each wing.

2. Sew around each wing piece, but leave the straight edge open. Sew with the edge of the presser foot on the edge of the fabric.

3.

Turn both wings right side out, and iron them. Fold in the open edges about ¼″, and iron them nice and flat.

4.

Position the wings on the sides of Olive's body, and carefully hand stitch them on. Don't forget to tie a knot at the beginning and at the end!

She is really starting to look like an owl, don't you think?

5.

Now let's sew on those cute little feet! Position them on the underside of Olive's body. Pin them in place. Using button thread, carefully sew them on. Sew along the straight edge of the feet only.

All done. I think she needs a friend, don't you? This is a great project to experiment with different fabrics and colors. Make it yours!

Mushroom Mansion

Finished size: 5˝ tall

what do I need?

- 9˝ × 12˝ sheets of wool felt in a variety of colors (You will need at least 3 sheets, and using more colors makes it more fun.)

- 1 baby sock (Save the second sock for another project or share it with a friend.)

- Fiberfill stuffing (Find it at a fabric store.)

- Rice

- Sewing machine

- Hot glue gun and gluestick

- Basic supplies (Refer to pages 12 and 14.)

special skills

- Using patterns (page 18)

- Whipstitch (page 20)

- Using a hot glue gun (page 22)

Prepare the pieces

Mushroom Mansion patterns are on pages 165 and 166.

1. Trace the pattern pieces onto parchment paper.

2. Choose the felt colors for each piece, and cut out the pieces. Cut out the center circle from only the bottom piece of the mushroom cap.

Let's make it!

STEM

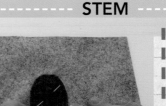

1.

Position the front door on the center of the mushroom base. Pin it in place.

EXTRA HELP

You may want to use fusible web to hold the pieces in place before you sew. If you do, see Using Fusible Web (page 19).

This little mushroom house is just the right size for some cute little backyard gnomes. **Wish I could make one my size!**

2.

With black thread, sew around the outside of the door. Sew some lines on the door, across and up and down. Copy the photo or make up your own design. Sew like a snail!

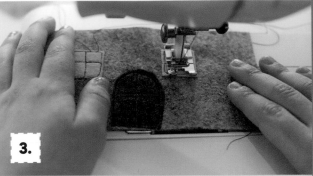

3.

Now do the same with the windows.

4.

Fold the stem of the mushroom in half, with right sides together. Pin it in place.

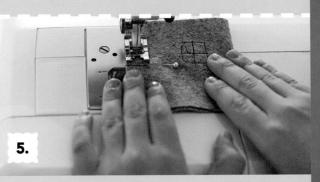

5.

Sew down the side with the edge of the presser foot on the edge of the felt. Turn the stem right side out.

6.

Position the round base on the bottom of the mushroom stem. Pin it in place as shown. It works best to pin the circle to the stem in quarters first; this will make it easier to evenly pin the base.

7.

Very carefully sew on the base using a whipstitch and button thread. Make your stitches small and close together.

8.

With help from an adult, fill the baby sock about three-fourths full with rice. Use a rolled-up piece of paper or a funnel.

9.

Tie a knot in the top of the sock.

10.

Drop the sock into the stem. Smoosh it around a bit so it isn't too lumpy and bumpy.

11.

Finish stuffing the stem with small tufts of fiberfill.

CAP

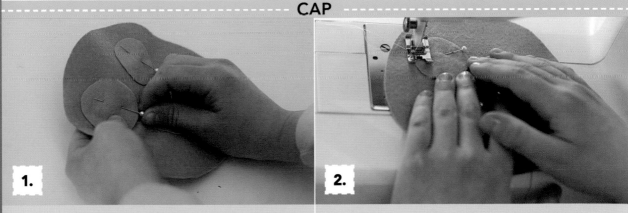

1.

Position the spots on the mushroom cap top. Pin them in place.

2.

Carefully sew around each spot. Sew close to the edge.

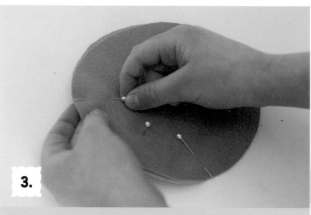

3.

Place the cap top and bottom right sides together, and pin.

4.

Sew with the edge of the presser foot on the edge of the felt all the way around the outside of the circle.

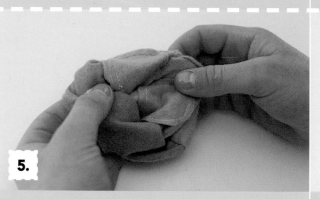

5.

Carefully pull the cap right side out through the hole. Wool felt *will* stretch, so be gentle!

6.

Gently stuff the cap with small tufts of fiberfill.

7.

Use your hot glue gun to add a line of glue around the very top of the stem.

8.

Place the stem inside the hole of the cap, and hold it firmly until the glue dries completely.

How cute are these little houses—don't you want a life-size version?

Basil and Midge

Finished size: 4½″ wide × 9″ tall

what do I need?

Makes 1 Basil or 1 Midge.

- Felt scraps for the face and base
- Felted sweater fabric (see How to Felt a Sweater, page 26) or ¼ yard wool felt for the body and arms
- Sleeve from another old sweater for the hat (Make sure the sleeve has a stretchy ribbed cuff.)
- 2 seed beads for the eyes
- Pom-pom for the hat
- 2 buttons for the arms
- Rice
- 1 baby sock (Save the second sock for another project or share it with a friend.)
- Fabric paint pen in light pink (Find this at a craft store.)
- Black button thread for the eyes and mouth
- White button thread
- Sewing machine
- Hot glue gun and gluestick
- Basic supplies (Refer to pages 12 and 14.)

special skills

- Using patterns (page 18)
- Using fusible web (page 19)
- Whipstitch (page 20)
- Using an iron (page 22)
- Using a hot glue gun (page 22)

Prepare the pieces

Basil and Midge patterns are on pages 163, 164, and 171.

1. Trace the patterns for Basil (or Midge) onto parchment paper.

2. Cut 2 body pieces from felted wool or wool felt.

3. Cut 1 felt circle for the base.

4. Cut 2 pieces of wool or felt for the arms.

5. Cut 2 pieces of wool or felt for the feet.

6. Cut 1 piece of felt for the face.

7. Cut 2 small circles of felt for the eyes.

Basil and Midge are a couple of friendly and curious little creatures who love to wander the woods in search of pinecones! Somehow Basil gets stuck doing all the work. That Midge is one bossy little critter!

FACE

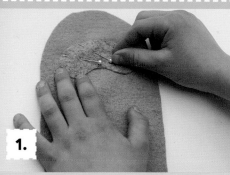

1.

Lay the felt face piece on top of the front body piece, and pin it in place. (See the pattern for placement.)

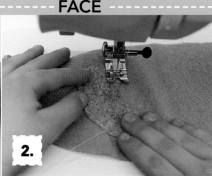

2.

Sew around the little face, staying nice and close to the edge.

EXTRA HELP

You may want to use fusible web to hold the face in place before you sew. If you do, see Using Fusible Web (page 19).

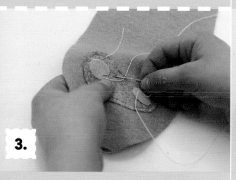

3.

Position the eye circles on the face. Pin, and sew them on with the machine or hand stitch. I like to hand stitch this part for a much neater look.

4.

Using black button thread, sew on the little seed bead eyes. Where you place the beads on the eye circles will help create your little creature's expression.

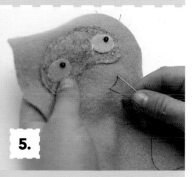

5.

For the mouth, make 1 long stitch using black thread. I went back and stitched over it a couple of times to make it stand out more.

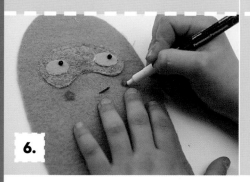

6.

For the cheeks, I used a fabric paint pen and colored some little circles. Let the paint dry. Then I gently ironed over the paint. (That will set the paint!)

1.

Place the front and back body pieces right sides together, and pin.

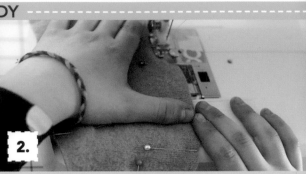

2.

With the edge of the presser foot on the edge of the wool or felt, sew around the body, leaving the bottom open. Backstitch at the beginning and end.

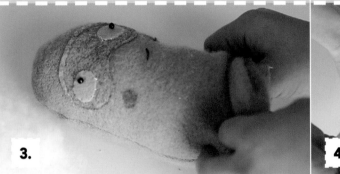

3.

Using small tufts of fiberfill, stuff your little creature about three-fourths full.

4.

Ask an adult to help you fill a baby sock with rice. Use a rolled-up piece of paper or a funnel. Tie a knot at the top of the sock to close it.

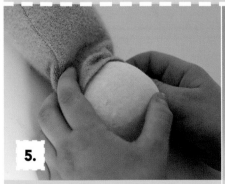

5.

Carefully put the sock into the body. Shape it so it isn't too lumpy and bumpy.

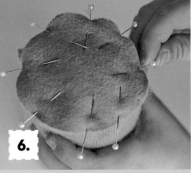

6.

Place the felt circle on the bottom of the body. Pin it in place.

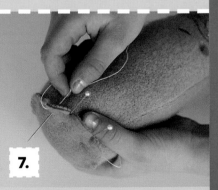

7.

Whipstitch all the way around the circle. Make your stitches nice and firm. Knot the end tightly.

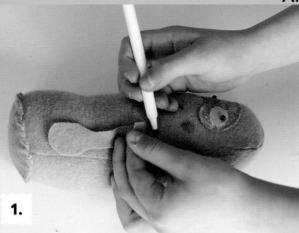

1.

Using your disappearing-ink fabric marker, mark the positions for the arms. Use the marks on the pattern piece as your guide. Pin the arms in place.

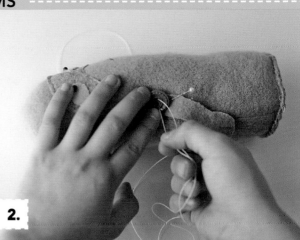

2.

Find the spot you marked for an arm, and, using button thread and a long needle, push the needle through Basil's (or Midge's) body and out to the other side (where you marked for the second arm). Leave a nice long tail! Push the needle through the second arm and a button, then bring the needle back down through another hole in the same button, and push it back through the body to the side where you started.

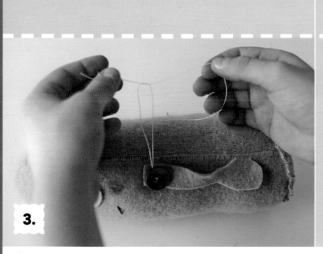

3.

Now sew through the arm and button on this side. This time bring the needle down through a hole in the button, but instead of passing it back through the body, bring the needle to the underside of that button. You will see the long tail still there, and this is where you can tie a nice tight double knot.

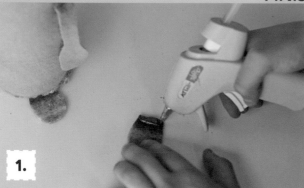

1.

Attach the feet with a little dab of hot glue. (Or you could sew the feet on instead.)

2.

Cut the cuff off an old sweater sleeve. This will be the hat. Cut it around 4˝ above the top of the ribbed cuff. Turn the cuff wrong side out and use a ruler to mark a diagonal line from the top of the cuff on one side to the top edge of the cut piece on the other side.

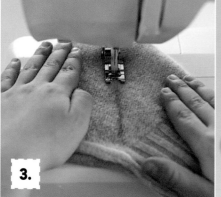

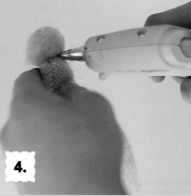

3.

Now sew along the marked line. This will give the hat that cute little point! Cut off the excess sleeve, and turn the hat right side out.

4.

Use hot glue to add a little pom-pom to the top of the hat. Stretch it a bit to fit it snugly on your creature's head.

Yahoo—you did it! Don't you want to make a whole family now?

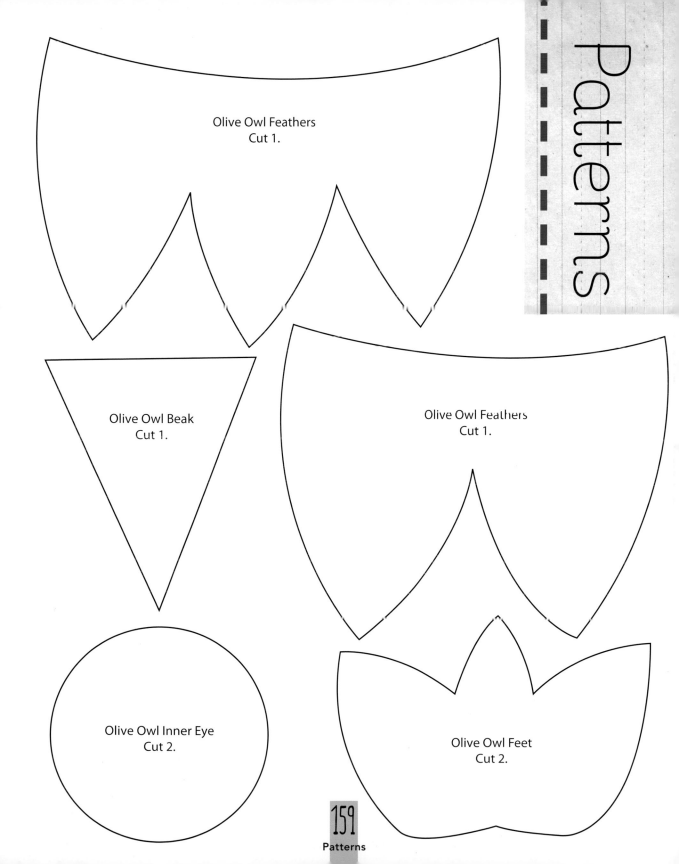

Olive Owl Feathers
Cut 1.

Olive Owl Beak
Cut 1.

Olive Owl Feathers
Cut 1.

Olive Owl Inner Eye
Cut 2.

Olive Owl Feet
Cut 2.

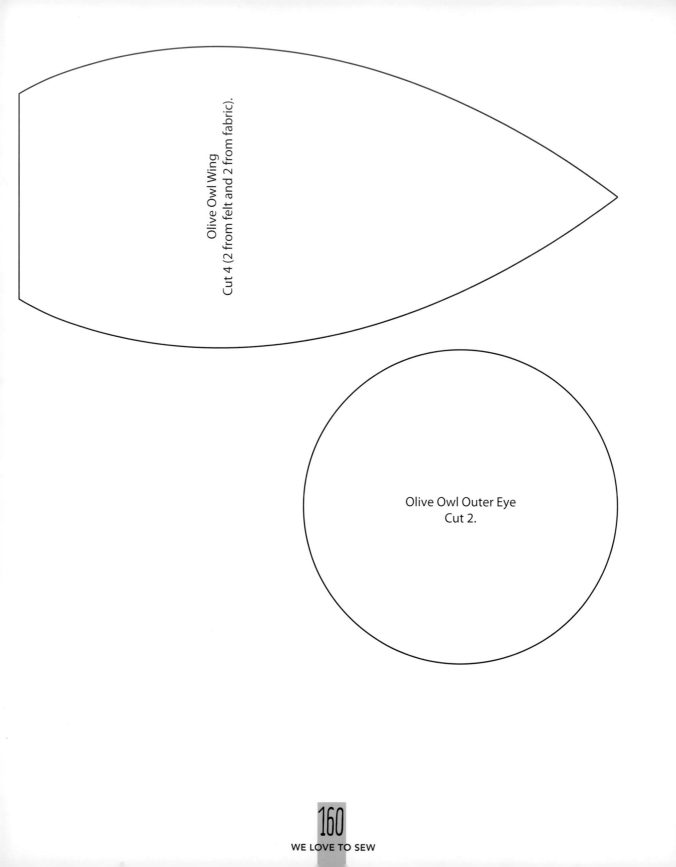

Olive Owl Wing
Cut 4 (2 from felt and 2 from fabric).

Olive Owl Outer Eye
Cut 2.

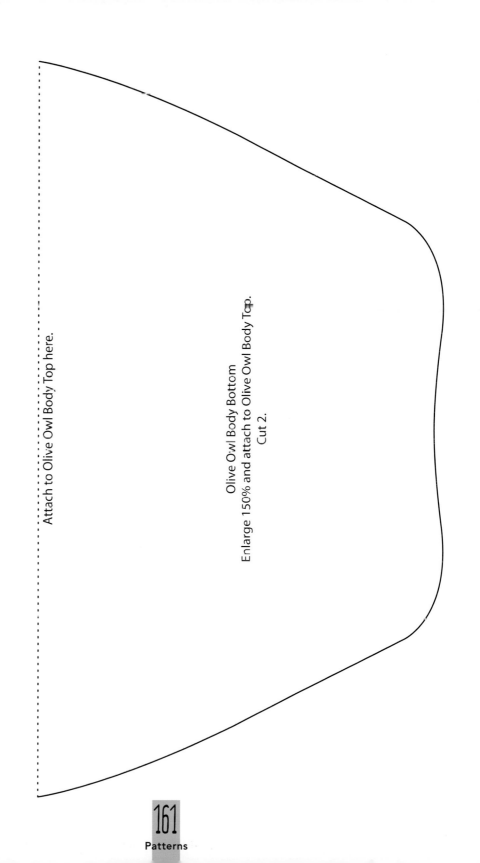

Attach to Olive Owl Body Top here.

Olive Owl Body Bottom
Enlarge 150% and attach to Olive Owl Body Top.
Cut 2.

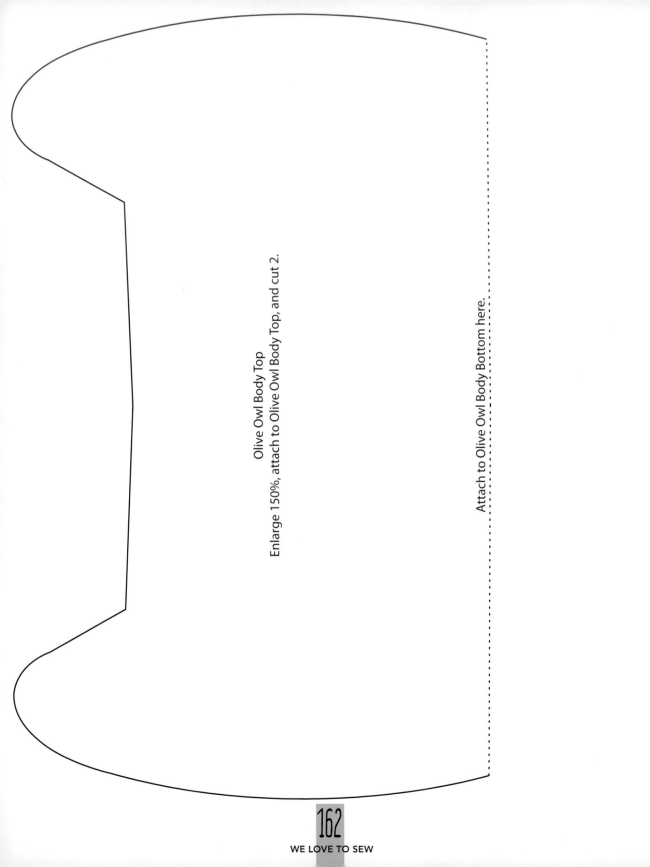

Olive Owl Body Top

Enlarge 150%, attach to Olive Owl Body Top, and cut 2.

Attach to Olive Owl Body Bottom here.

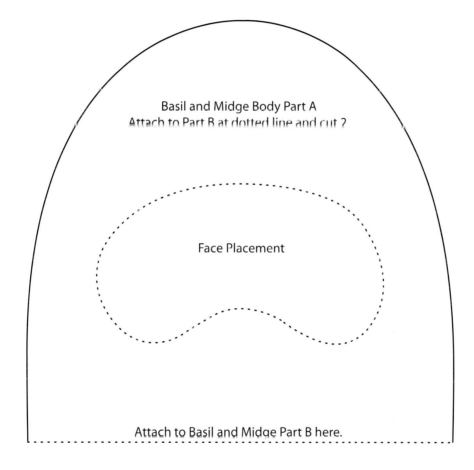

Basil and Midge Body Part A
Attach to Part B at dotted line and cut 2

Face Placement

Attach to Basil and Midge Part B here.

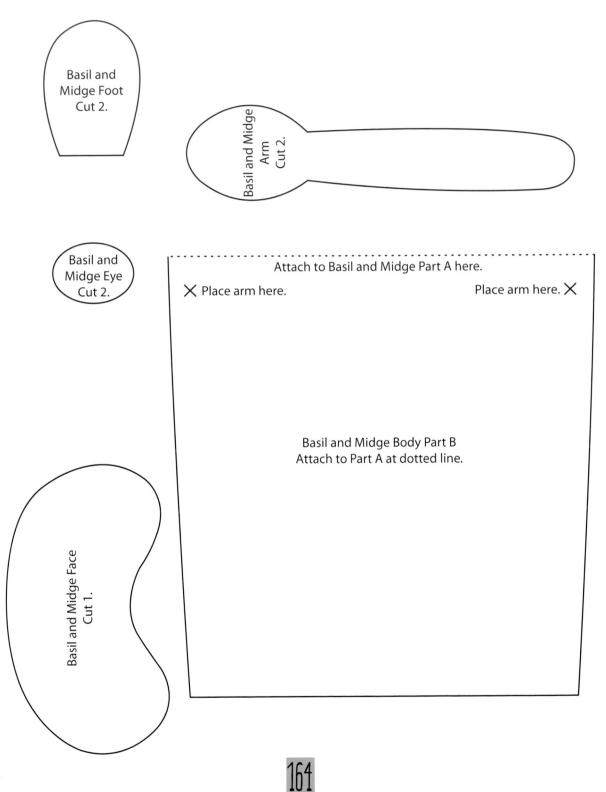

Basil and Midge Foot Cut 2.

Basil and Midge Arm Cut 2.

Basil and Midge Eye Cut 2.

Attach to Basil and Midge Part A here.

✕ Place arm here.

Place arm here. ✕

Basil and Midge Body Part B
Attach to Part A at dotted line.

Basil and Midge Face Cut 1.

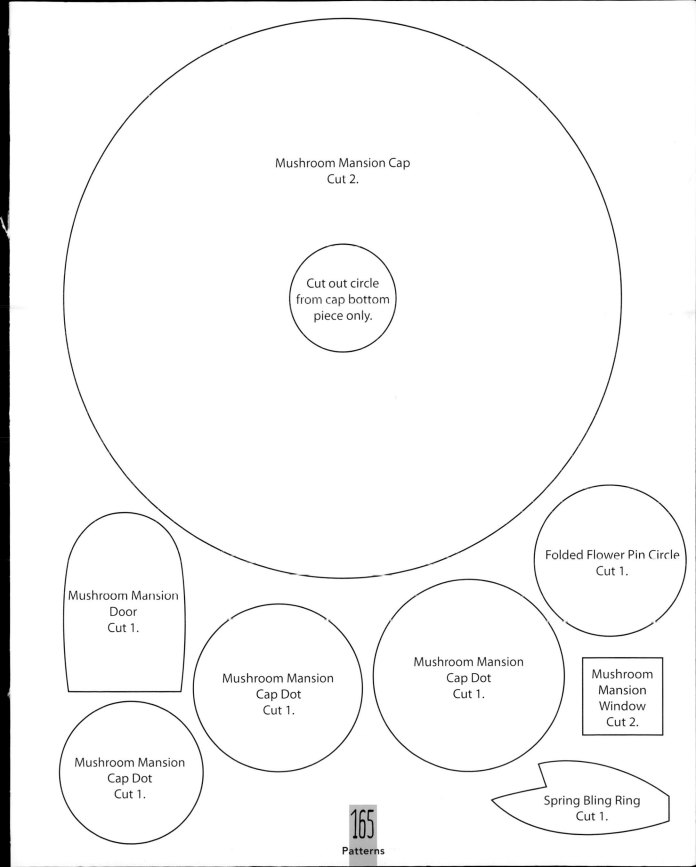

Mushroom Mansion Cap
Cut 2.

Cut out circle
from cap bottom
piece only.

Folded Flower Pin Circle
Cut 1.

Mushroom Mansion
Door
Cut 1.

Mushroom Mansion
Cap Dot
Cut 1.

Mushroom Mansion
Cap Dot
Cut 1.

Mushroom
Mansion
Window
Cut 2.

Mushroom Mansion
Cap Dot
Cut 1.

Spring Bling Ring
Cut 1.

165
Patterns

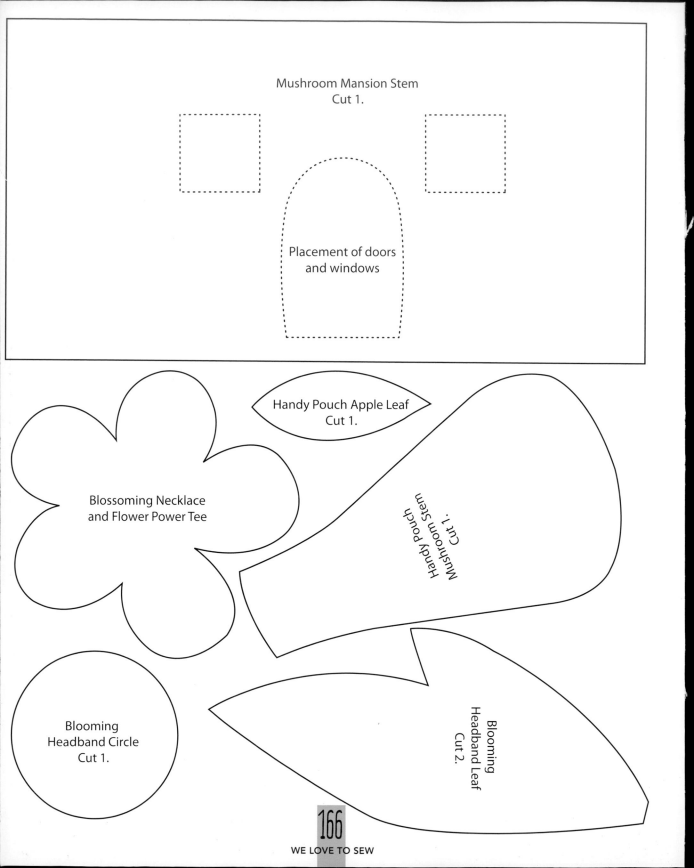

Mushroom Mansion Stem
Cut 1.

Placement of doors
and windows

Handy Pouch Apple Leaf
Cut 1.

Blossoming Necklace
and Flower Power Tee

Handy Pouch
Mushroom Stem
Cut 1.

Blooming
Headband Circle
Cut 1.

Blooming
Headband Leaf
Cut 2.

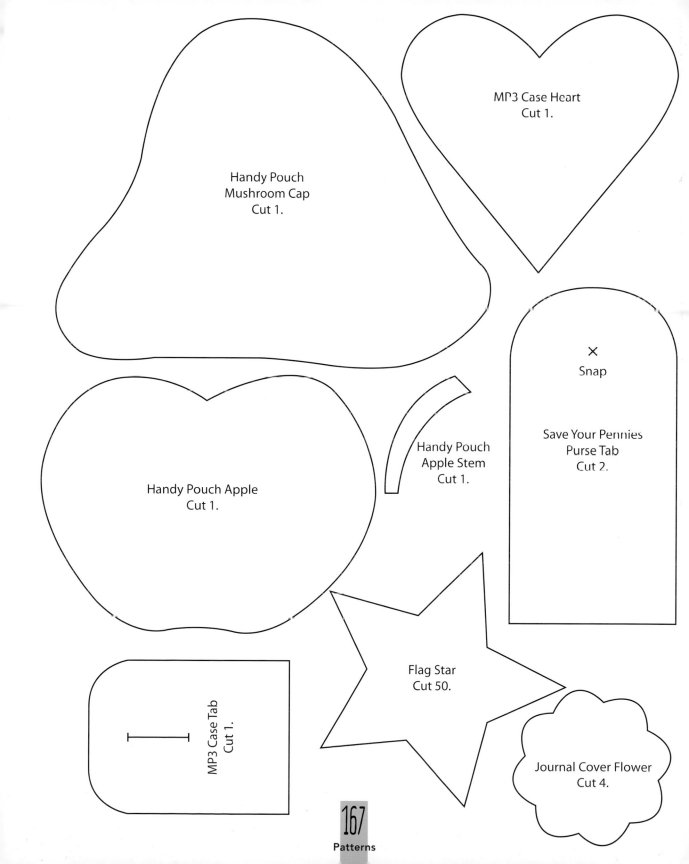

MP3 Case Heart
Cut 1.

Handy Pouch
Mushroom Cap
Cut 1.

Save Your Pennies
Purse Tab
Cut 2.

✕
Snap

Handy Pouch
Apple Stem
Cut 1.

Handy Pouch Apple
Cut 1.

Flag Star
Cut 50.

MP3 Case Tab
Cut 1.

Journal Cover Flower
Cut 4.

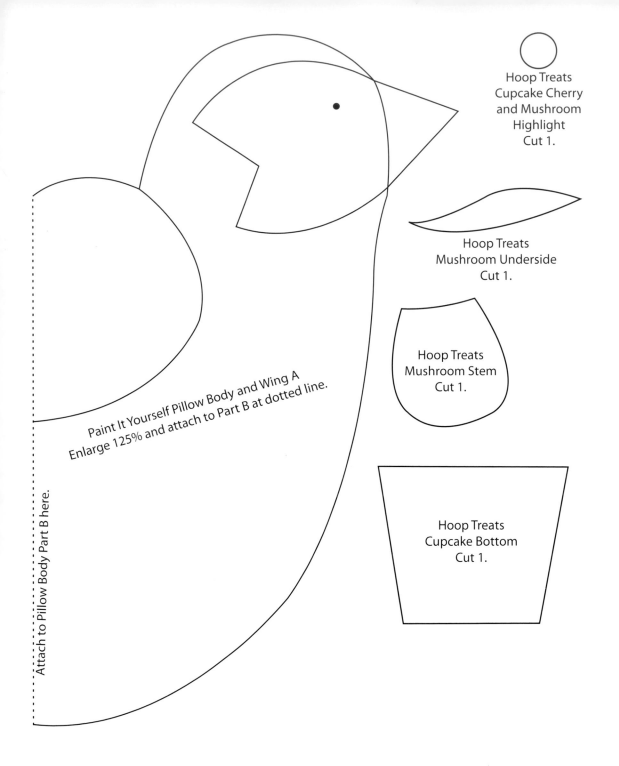

Hoop Treats
Cupcake Cherry
and Mushroom
Highlight
Cut 1.

Hoop Treats
Mushroom Underside
Cut 1.

Hoop Treats
Mushroom Stem
Cut 1.

Hoop Treats
Cupcake Bottom
Cut 1.

Paint It Yourself Pillow Body and Wing A
Enlarge 125% and attach to Part B at dotted line.

Attach to Pillow Body Part B here.

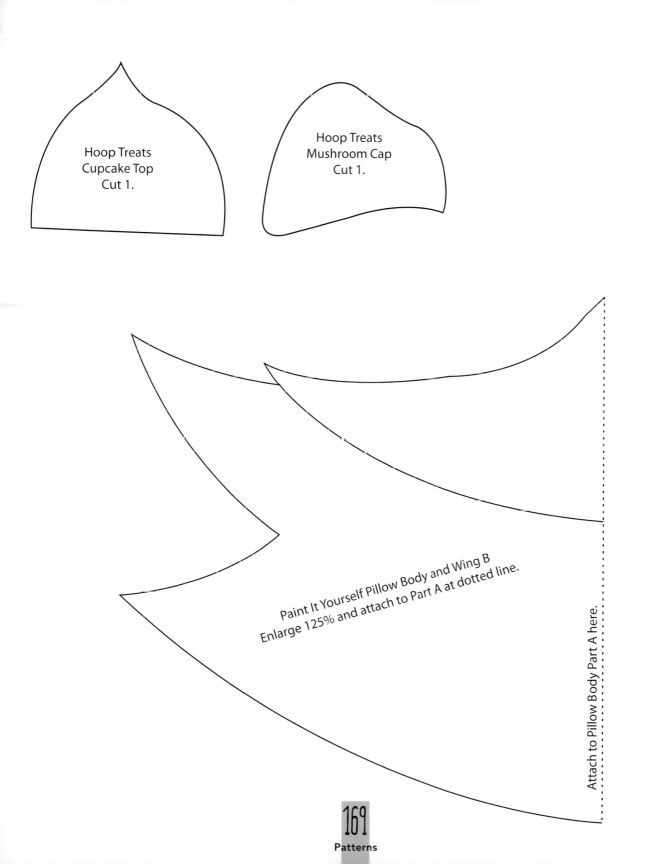

Hoop Treats
Cupcake Top
Cut 1.

Hoop Treats
Mushroom Cap
Cut 1.

Paint It Yourself Pillow Body and Wing B
Enlarge 125% and attach to Part A at dotted line.

Attach to Pillow Body Part A here.

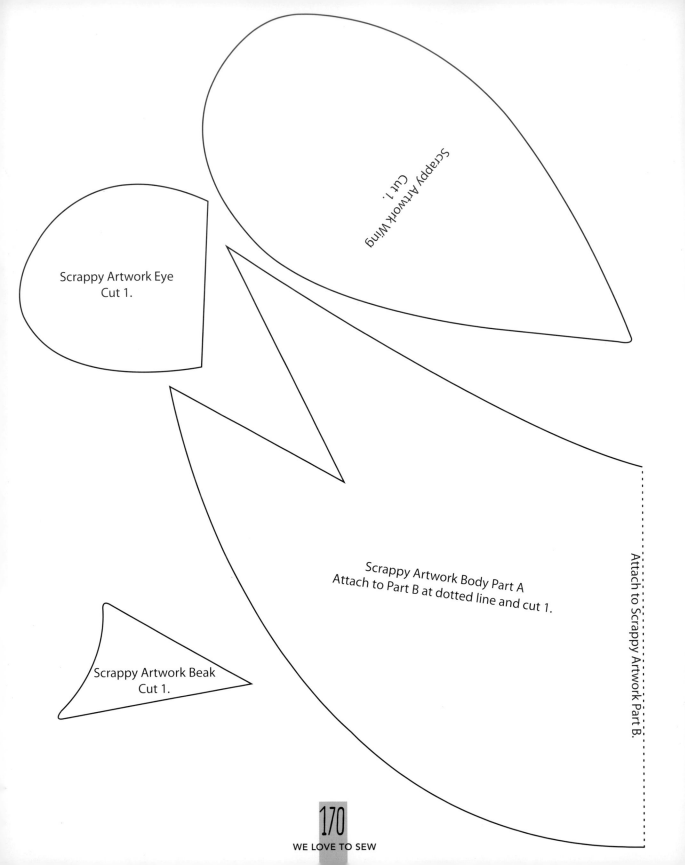

Scrappy Artwork Wing
Cut 1.

Scrappy Artwork Eye
Cut 1.

Scrappy Artwork Body Part A
Attach to Part B at dotted line and cut 1.

Attach to Scrappy Artwork Part B.

Scrappy Artwork Beak
Cut 1.

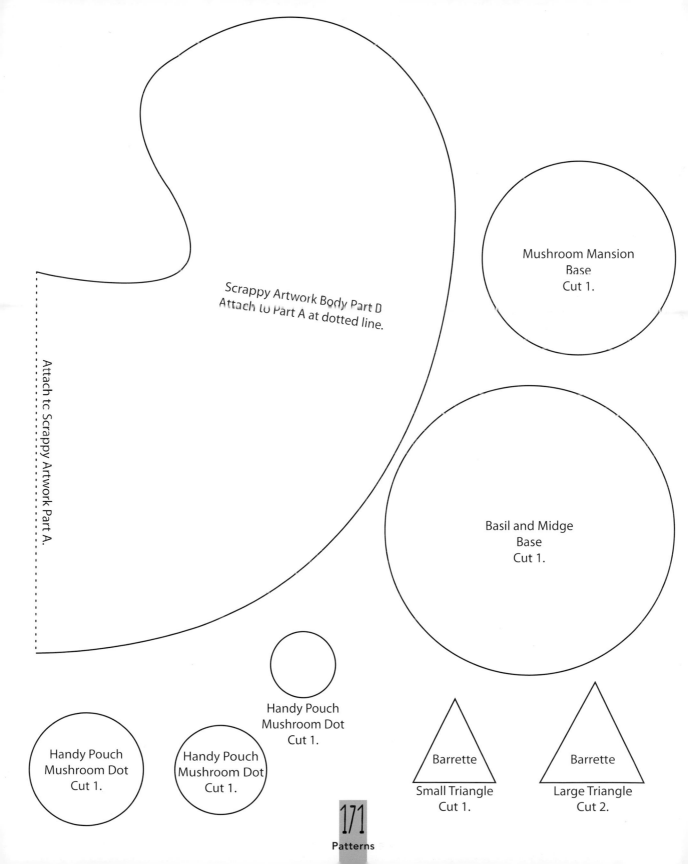

Scrappy Artwork Body Part D
Attach to Part A at dotted line.

Attach to Scrappy Artwork Part A.

Mushroom Mansion
Base
Cut 1.

Basil and Midge
Base
Cut 1.

Handy Pouch
Mushroom Dot
Cut 1.

Handy Pouch
Mushroom Dot
Cut 1.

Handy Pouch
Mushroom Dot
Cut 1.

Barrette
Small Triangle
Cut 1.

Barrette
Large Triangle
Cut 2.

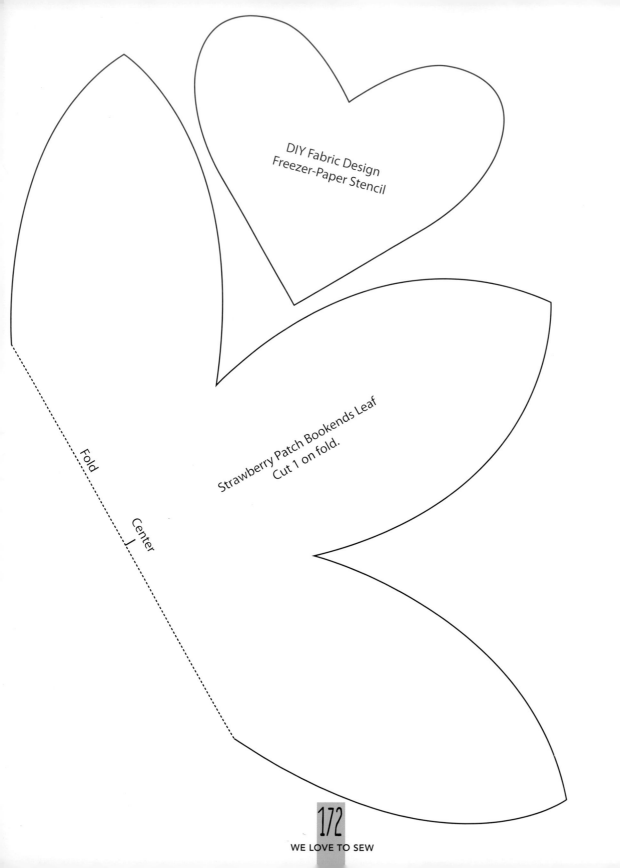

DIY Fabric Design
Freezer-Paper Stencil

Strawberry Patch Bookends Leaf
Cut 1 on fold.

Fold

Center

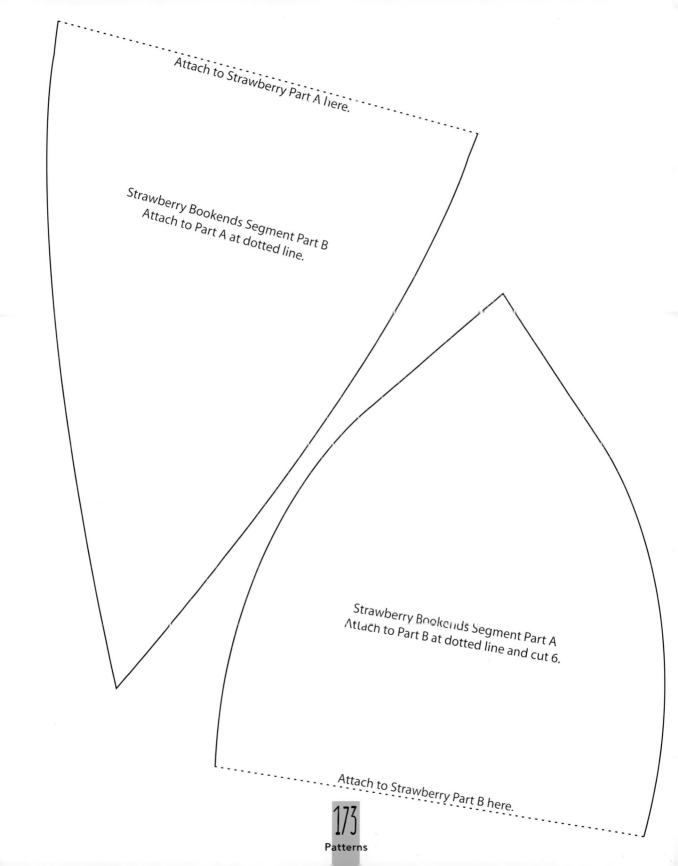

Attach to Strawberry Part A here.

Strawberry Bookends Segment Part B
Attach to Part A at dotted line.

Strawberry Bookends Segment Part A
Attach to Part B at dotted line and cut 6.

Attach to Strawberry Part B here.

Resources

Shops and websites that I love to visit

Fabric.com   fabric.com

Fabricworm   fabricworm.com

Hancock Fabrics   hancockfabrics.com

Hawthorne Threads   hawthornethreads.com

Jo-Ann   joann.com

Michaels   michaels.com

Purl Soho   purlsoho.com

Oh-so-helpful companies

Birch Fabrics   birchfabrics.com

Clothfabric (Australia)   clothfabric.com

DecoArt   decoart.com

Lion Brand Yarn   lionbrand.com

National Nonwovens   woolfelt.com

Timeless Treasures Fabrics   ttfabrics.com

Look for your local shops!

Where would we be without our local stores? My favorites near my home in Virginia are Kelly Ann's Quilting, 145 Art and Design Studio, Fabric Emporium, and The Red Thread.

About Little Pincushion Studio

When my daughter was seven years old, she took a piece of fabric and a roll of tinfoil and made herself a rather fetching outfit. I was amazed that she could look at this piece of cloth and visualize what it was to become. And who knew that tinfoil is perfect for making shoes!

It was the perfect time to introduce her to the magical wonders of sewing and creativity. I taught her the basics of how to use the sewing machine and just let her go for it. Her sense of pride and accomplishment were so great to witness, and her crazy use of color and pattern made me swoon.

I started thinking that teaching little girls could be fun. Of course, the basics are really important. But so is the fun of experimentation and tackling unusual and original projects. Little Pincushion Studio was a natural progression of my thinking.

You can visit my website at littlepincushionstudio.com.

In my studio, girls love learning how to sew the most wonderful and creative things!

About the Author

Annabel is a crafty mom from Australia who now lives in the Virginia countryside. She owns Little Pincushion Studio, where she teaches girls everything they need to know to go forth and conquer the world of sewing and creating.

Annabel writes a blog by the same name, where she shares all her daily inspirations, crafty ventures, and thrifty purchases. She lives in her little house with her husband, Darren; her children, Oliver and Ruby; and a very loud, snoring pug named Coco.